1784 Tax Lists

of

Somerset County

and

Worcester County

Maryland

Compiled by:
Ruth T. Dryden

Southern Historical Press, Inc.
Greenville, South Carolina

This volume was reproduced
from a personal copy located in
the Publishers private library

Please direct all correspondence and book orders to:
SOUTHERN HISTORICAL PRESS, Inc.
PO Box 1267
Greenville, SC   29602-1267

ISBN #978-1-63914-238-5
Printed in the United States of America

1783 Tax lists of Somerset County

By Joseph Cottman, assessor of Wicomico District

OWNERS NAME	LAND	TOTAL ACRES	White Inhab. MALE-FEMALE
JOHN ADAMS SR.	Andrews Dissappointemnt 91/23a. Dashiells Lott 10a. Tonys Vine-Yard 84a. Horseys Chance 101a. Cramburn 215a. Wilsons Folly 50a. Wallers Chance 36a. Glasgow Swamp 265a. Johns Desire 82a. Adams Discovery 188½a. Young Tinson 1a. Beretons Chance 10a. Winder 13/4a. White Chappel 1a.	1646½a.	3 - 2
JOHN ADAMS JR.	Adams Chance 40a.	40a.	0 - 0
WILLIAM ADAMS	Wallers Chance 212a. Cramburn 37a. Trouble 201a. Windsor 30¼a. Mill Lott 91½a.	566½a.	1 - 1
ANDREW ADAMS	Smiths adventure 260a. Clover ground 45½a. Turkey Trap Ridge 30a. White Chappel 100a. Adams Purchase 48a. This or None 49½a.	445½a.	3 - 2
JOSIAH ADAMS	Windsor 184a. Daintree 150a. Trouble 250a. Swamp 30a.	420a.	2 - 2
STEPHEN ADAMS	Double Purchase 286½a. Gernsee (Gernsey) 150a.	435½a.	2 - 6
ELIJAH AUSTIN	Austins Security 60½a.	60½a.	2 - 2
JOHN AUSTIN	Fish Neck 50a.	50a.	3 - 2
HAMILTON AUSTIN	Mill Security ½a.	½a.	3 - 2
JAMES ANDERSON	Poor Quarter 50a. Do.Better 13½a.	63½a.	5 - 4
WILLIAM ALLEN	Fortune 60a. Sligo Little Beleane 471a.	531½a.	4 - 4
CHARLES BALLARD	Hazzard 200a.	200a.	2 - 1
CHARLES BALLARD JR.	----		2 - 1
BENJAMIN BAILEY	Baileys Craft 40½a.	40½a	1 - 0
MATILDA BOUNDS	Bounds Chance 237½a. Chance 10a.	267½a.	2 - 2
JONES BOUNDS	Stephens Lott 70a. Addition 92a.	162a.	2 - 3
ROBERT BANKS	Roberts Security 301a.	301a.	5 - 3
GEORGE BAILEY JR.	End of Strife 2a. Baileys Chance 41a. Taylors Good Luck 25a. What You Please 57a. Harman 75a. land escheated from Glouster 60a.	267a.	2 - 2
MILLS BAILEY	Baileys Purchase 50a. Baines Addition 52a.	103a.	4 - 3
STEPHEN BAYNS	Widows Hope 13a. What you Please 3a.	16a.	3 - 4
HENRY BANKS	Last Choice 24½a. Brittiane 50a. Howards Discovery 57a.	131½a.	4 - 4
THOMAS BEARD	Laytons Discovery 100a.	100a.	2 - 2
WILLIAM BING	Salisblry Survey (town)	3/4a.	2 - 2
WILLIAM BRERETON	Smiths Adventure 67a. Mile End 13a. Breretons Chance 100a.	219a.	4 - 0

By Joseph C₀ttman, assessor Wicomico District

OWNERS NAME	LAND	Total Acres	White Inhab. Males-Females
JAMES BENNETT	Havanna 200a. Crouches Desire 50a.	250a.	0 - 0
JOHN BROWN	Green Briar 77½a.	77½a.	0 - 0
JOHN CHRISTOPHER	Monsham 95a.	95a.	2 - 5
THOMAS COLLINS	Stevens Conquest 244a. Stephens Folly 22a.	266a.	2 - 6
WILLIAM COLLINS	none		1 - 1
WILLIAM CALLAHAN	none		2 - 3
RACHEL CHAMBERS	Josephs Beginning 102a. Layfields Chance 124a.	226a.	2 - 4
EUNICE COLLINS	Morris Purchase 100a.	100a.	1 - 2
STEPHEN CHRISTOPHER	Mill Security 3/4a.	3/4a.	2 - 2
THOMAS COX Sr.	Plumptons Salt Ash 30a. Wilton 50a.	80a.	4 - 2
JOHN CHITTAM	Do Better 2½a. Buttocking Ridge 151a. Castle Haven 50a.	203½a.	4 - 3
WALKER CHITTAM	none		2 - 2
THOMAS COX Jr.	Cox's Fork 8¼a. Middle Neck 48a. Smiths Chance 98a. Wheel of Fortune 6¼a. Cox's Fork 98a.	240 3/4a.	7 - 4
CLARKSON COX	Plumpton Saltash 50a.	50a.	2 - 1
SAMUEL COVINGTON	Horseys Bailywick 186½a. Little Belan 454a. Phillips Addition 25a. Lowes Enlarged	573½a.	1 - 1
SARAH COLLETT	none		0 - 1
BENJAMIN COTTMAN	Young Tinson 13a. Tinson In Indian 150a. Taunton Deane ? Cottmans Venture 52a. Cottmans Freehold 18a. Cottmans Purchase 31a. ----	419a.	2 - 1
ALEXANDER CHANE	Support 50a. Adams Chance 50a.	100a.	3 - 5
WILLIAM DOCKERY	Ferry Hill 17¼a. Marsh Pasture 10 3/4a. Last Purchase 10a.	38a.	1 - 5
MARY DISHAROON	Ascues Choice 58a.	58a.	0 - 1
JESSE DORMAN	Gulletts Hope 50a. Peter Hill	85a.	1 - 0
CONSTANT DISHAROON	White Chappel 30a. Satisfied 74a. Hopkins Lott 21½a. Will Have More 100a. Good Luck 50a. Come no Nigher 50a.	375a.	1 - 2
JOHN DORMAN	Dormans Conclusion 139a. Hunting Quarter 26a.	165a.	3 - 5
WILLIAM DISHAROON	Second Purchase 50a. Would have Had More 50a.	200a.	2 - 3
THOMAS DASHIELL	Dashiells Lott 100a. Island Marsh 17½a. Point of Marsh 9¼a.	126½a.	0 - 0
JOSIAH DASHIELL	Dashiells Lott 425a. Chance 15a.	440a.	2 - 3
FRANCIS DISHAROON	Havannah 100a. Watsons Discovery 140a.		2 - 5
JOSEPH DASHIELL	none		0 - 0
GEORGE DISHAROON	Watsons Discovery 60a. Shave the Bald Friar 72a. Addition 22½a.	154½a.	0 - 0
MARY DISHAROON	Frizzles Enjoyment 150a.	150a.	0 - 3

By Joseph Cottman, assessor of Wicomico District

OWNERS NAME	LAND	TOTAL ACRES	WHITE INHAB. MALE-FEMALE
JAMES DISHEROON	Come No Nigher 118a.	118a.	4 - 3
JOSHUA DISHAROON	Hopkins Lott 168½a.	168½a.	1 - 0
STEPHEN DISHAROON	Ascues Choice 160a. Come Between 20½a.	180½a.	1 - 5
NEWTON DISHAROON	Good Intention	177a.	1 - 2
JOHN DASHIELL	Sligo Little Balean	100a.	0 - 0
WILLIAM DAILY	Layfields Chance	19a.	2 - 2
STEPHEN DUTTON	(11) Mason	100a.	0 - 0
WILLIAM DYMOCK	Mill Security	1½a.	3 - 3
ROBERT DASHIELL	Mill Security 3/4a. Havannah 289½a. Mill Lott 30½a.	320¼a.	2 - 4
BENJAMIN DASHIELL	none		0 - 0
DONNOCK DENNIS	Pembertons Good Will (faded)		2 - 2
MATHIAS DASHIELL	Dashiells Lott- Chance (faded)		1 - 0
GEORGE DASHIELL	Stephens Folly 20a, What you Please, Whittys Later Invention Conclusion	535½a.	3 - 2
ANN ELZEY	Second Purchase 350a. Ellis Chance 100a. Elzeys Choice 100a.	350½a.	4 - 3
JOSEPH FOWLER	none		5 - 2
EDWARD FOWLER	Lotts Daughter, Lotts Son	237a.	3 - 2
THOMAS FOUNTAIN	Cramburn, Horseys Chance 78a. Canterbury 87a.	190a.	3 - 1
HENRY FITZGERALD	Lowes Enlarged	103 3/4a.	1-1
THOMAS GILLES	End of Strife	283a.	2 - 4
LEVIN GILLIS	Meadow 21½a. Support 58a. End of Strife 125a.	281½a.	0 - 0
MARY GILLIS	none		0 - 0
SARAH GILLIS	none		0 - 0
SALATHIEL GRIFFITH	Little Belane	150a.	5 - 3
JOHN GOSLEE	Goslees Lott	158a.	6 - 3
GEORGE GOSLEE	none		1 - 1
JOSEPH GILLIS	White Chappel 167a. Gillis's Double Purchase 303a. End of Strife 80a. Cranburn 30½a.	995 3/4a.	3- 5
ABRAHAM GULLETT	Mills Security 1a.	1a.	1 - 2
LEVIN GUNBY	Thomas's Conclusion 143a. Stanfords Finding 21a. Crooked Lane 31a.	262½a.	5 - 5
LEVIN GALE	Last Purchase 60a. Coxes Lott 160a.		0 - 0
JOSEPH GOSLEE	Sligo 50a. Hogridge 41a. Goslees Lott 35a. Goslees Chance 25¼a.	150¼a.	2 - 2
TEMPY HARRIS	Lott	166a.	2 - 3
MARY HARRIS	Lott 83a.	83a.	0 - 2
JOHN HARRIS	Lott 200a.	200a.	5 - 5
THOMAS HOLBROOK	Last Vacancy 60a. Flowerfield 115½a. Conclusion 652a. Last Purchase 252a.	920½a.	4 - 3
JOSHUA HILMAN	Last Choice 100a. Hilman's First Choice 34½a.	134½a.	3 - 3

By Joseph Cottman, assessor of Wicomico District

OWNERS NAME	LAND	TOTAL ACRES	White Inhab. MALE-FEMALE
BETTY HILMAN	Buading 50a.	50a.	3 - 3
REVEL HAYMAN	New Addition 13½a. Charles Chance 20a. High Meadow 63½a.	96a.	2 - 4
LYDIA HAYMAN	none		0 - 1
JOHN H. HAYMAN	Addition 60a. Hopewell 56a.	116a.	3 - 2
JOSHUA HAYMAN	White Oak Swamp 18a. Wolfspitt Ridge Addition 270a.	288a.	1 - 0
ISAAC HAYMAN	Wolfspitt Ridge 70a. Haymans Purchase, Addition	122a.	2 - 3
JAMES HILL	Manor Land 65a.	65a.	1 - 4
JOSHUA HUMPHRIES	Hogsdown 170a.	170a.	4 - 7
EBENEZER HANDY	Wilton 10a. Alderbury	80a.	0 - 0
BENJAMIN HITCH	Mount Pleasant	100a.	4 - 4
Dr. JAMES HOUSTON	Mill Security ½a.	½a.	4 - 0
FREDERICK HILL	none		5 - 3
WILLIAM HILL	none		6 - 2
BENJAMIN HENDERSON	Never Out Done 10a. Fitchwaters Study 350a.	360a.	0 - 0
BETTY HAYMAN	Hopewell 30a. Addition 53a.	73a.	3 - 0
WILLIAM HORSEY	none		0 - 0
JOHN JONES	2nd. Addition to Hog Quarter	170a.	0 - 0
JOHN JEANNOR	Gillis's Meadow	50a.	2 - 2
EZEKIEL JENKINS	Poor Shad Point	50a.	1 - 1
FRANCIS JONES	Second Purchase	100a.	2 - 2
DAVID JENKINS	Hogneck 100a.	100a.	3 - 5
JAMES JONES	none		2 - 4
SAMUEL INGERSOLL	Fathers Care 161a. Addition 30a. Venture 50a. Middle 11½a.	266 3/4a.	3 - 5
JOHN JENKINS	Crouches Desire 50a.	50a.	3 - 2
KIBBLE JENKINS	Hoggs Neck 250a. Hobs Dissapointment 20½a. Good Increase 4½a.	275a.	2 - 3
JONATHAN KNIGHT	Knights Discovery 50a.	50a.	2 - 2
BETTY KIBBLE	Security	113a.	3 - 2
JOHN C. KILBYS heirs	Security	100a.	0 - 0
ROBERT LEATHERBURY	Covingtons Folly 70a. My own Before 61a. Lott 200a.	351a.	3 - 3
ROBERT LAYFIELD	Lott	80½a.	1 - 2
FRANCIS LANK	Batchelors Folly	106½a.	1 - 2
HENRY LURTEN	Toadvines Adventure	70a.	3 - 5
ELISHA LAWRENCE	Susans Luck	30a.	2 - 2
JOSEPH LEONARD	Cordwinders Hall 18¼a. Cox's Advice 50a. Levins Chance 50a. Johnsons Lott 39½a. Gash 40a. Plumptons Salt Ash 40a.	212a.	5 - 1
JOHN LEONARD	Holders Chance 65a. Cox's Fork 140a.		2 - 1
REBECCA LEVINS	none		0 - 1
GEORGE LAYFIELD	none		1 - 1
HENRY LOWES	Hereafter 200a. Fathers Care 120a. Dispence 200a. Security 153½a. Priviledge 8a. Robinsons Lott 300a. Grog 49½a. Ralphs Prevention 9a. Green Hammock 134 3/4a. Addition to Lowes Point 15a. -----	1079a.	1 - 2

By Joseph Cottman, Assessor of Wicomico District

OWNERS NAME	LAND	TOTAL ACRES	White Inhab. MALE-FEMALE
ALEXANDER McLAUGHLEN	Norths Situation	436a.	2 - 2
JOSEPH MORRIS	Goddards Folly 90a. North Situation 25a. Morris's Resolution 9½a.	101a.	2 - 3
JOHN MORRIS	none		1 - 1
MARY MALONE	Malones Venture 20 2/4a. Turkey Ridge 83 3/4a.	103 2/4a.	1- 2
JOSEPH MITCHELL	Ballys Chance 50a.	50a.	5 - 2
JOHN MADDUX Jr.	Second Purchase 50a.	50a.	2 - 3
MATHIAS MILES	First Conclusion 92a. Last Conclusion 152a. Mathias Choice 70a.	314a.	0 - 0
WILLIAM McBRYDE	Mill Security ¼a.	¼a.	0 - 0
JAMES McLEARY	Mill Security ¼a.	¼a.	2 - 4
ROBERT MALONE	Goddards Folly 100a. Malones Lott 79½a. Robins Lott 74½a. name unknown	227a.	6 - 2
JACOB MORRIS	Come by Chance 100a.	100a.	6 - 1
JOHN MADDUX Jr.	Cox's Fork 75a.	75a.	0 - 0
SARAH NEWMAN	Newmans Meadow 52¼a. Bottom of The Neck 80a. Newmans Conclusion 100a.	230½a.	2 - 4
BENJAMIN NUTTER	Jacobs ? Point 28½a.	28½a.	1 - 3
JOHN NELMS	Pemberton Good Will 10a. Plumpston Salt Ash 10a. Mill Security 1a. Wheel of Fortune 15a. Adams His Brother 30a.	64a.	5 - 3
JOHN ORPHANT	none		4 - 2
SAMUEL PRICE	Addition and Union??	201a.	1 - 2
JOSIAH POLK	Hopewell 300a. Do Better 50a. Hogsdown 100a. Comly Chance 100a. Gristy? 30a. Buttocking Ridge 304½a. Fortune 230a. Forceput 50a. Buttocking Ridge 120a. Hogdon 30a. Do Better ¼a. name unknwn	1485¼a.	1 - 0
DAVID PRIOR	Back Swamp 91½a. Taylors Priviledge 85½a. Double Purchase	201¼a.	1 - 4
GILLIS POLK	Fathers Care 283½a. Roxburg 210a. Priviledge 50a.	625½a.	2 - 4
JOSIAH & GILLIS POLK	Partners Good Luck 50a.	50a.	0 - 0
THOMAS POLLITT	Dentry 50a. Trouble 20a. Johns Hill 12a. FoxHall 56a.	228a.	3 - 3
JONATHAN POLLITT	Long Ridge 125a. Tamroons Ridge 50a. Addition to Tamroons Ridge 21½a.	196½a.	4 - 1
JOHN PULLET Jr.	High Meadow 150a.	150a.	2 - 1
JONATHAN POLLITT Jr.	Bayns Addition 4½a. Cock-More 140a.	144½a.	2 - 1
GEORGE POLLITT Sr.	Smithfield 100a. CHOICE 37a. Addition to Tamroons Ridge 172½a. name unknown 14a.	323½a.	4 - 4
JOHN PARKER(of George)	Newberry 50a. Plumptons Salt Ash 35a.Parkers Chance	125a.	0 - 0
GEORGE POLLITT Jr.	none		1 - 0

By Joseph Cottman, Assessor of the Wicomico District

OWNERS NAME	LAND	TOTAL ACRES	WHITE INHAB. MALE-FEMALE
JAMES POLK	Eswicks?? Chance 50a.	50a.	1 - 1
WILLIAM POLK	Robertsons Lott 285½a. Cow Pasture 38a. Williams Lott	319½a.	4 - 3
JOHN REDDISH JR.	none		1 - 2
THOMAS RENCHER	Renchers Security 100a. Covingtons Meadpw 105a. Addn. to Covingtons Meadow 33 /34a. Earlndy 149a. Addition 66a. Ignoble 32a. Whittys Convience 50a.	626½a.	6 - 5
HIRON REDDISH	Does Better 160½a. Plain Dealing 50a.	210½a.	2 - 2
JOHN REDDISH JR.	Castle Haven 35a. Plain Dealing 222a. Addn. to Plain Dealing 11a. ? Gate 218½a.	218½a.	6 - 1
RICHARD RICHARDS	Mill Security 1a.	1a.	1 - 1
JAMES ROCK	Addition to Mullen Field 50a. Greenbriar 96¼a.	146¼a.	0 - 0
NICHOLAS REDDISH	Reddish's Lott 50a. Addition to Reddish's Lott 29¼a.	79¼a.	4 - 7
WILLIAM SUTTON	none		2 - 4
GEORGE SHARP	Tower Hill 160a. Shave the Bald Friar 54a.	214a.	4 - 2
GEORGE SIRMAN	Isaacs Choice	39½a.	1 - 4
GRACE SIRMAN	Isaacs Choice	45½a.	2 - 3
GEORGE SOCKWELL	Hales's Folly	33½a.	2 - 3
EDWARD SIRMAN	Fountains Frolick	96½a.	3 - 2
JOSHUA STANFORD	Little Neck	100a.	4 - 3
SAMUEL SOCKWELL	Fox Island 67a. Hound Ridge	100a.	4 - 3
JONATHAN STANFORD	Turners Choice 75a. Stanfords Finding 11½a.	86½a.	2 - 1
DAVID STANFORD	Little Neck 120¼a. What you Please 69a.	189½a.	5 - 6
THOMAS SKINNER	Pembertons Good Will ½a. Smiths Chance 23a.	23½a.	5 - 1
GEORGE STEVENS	Mill Security ½a.	½a.	1 - 0
ARCHIBALD SMITH	Plumpton Saltash 100a. Cordwinders Lott 25a.	125a.	4 - 2
JOHN SMITH	Plumpton Saltash 100a. Cordwinders Lott 25a.	125a.	1 - 0
JOHN SHILES	Little Belane 163a. Allens Dissappointment 9a.	172a.	3 - 1
THOMAS SHILES	none		1 - 0
EPHRAIM STEVENS	Jennors Good Luck 50a.	50a.	4 - 4
JOSHUA STURGIS	pt. Addition	100a.	0 - 0
ARCHIBALD SMITH	Wheel of Fortune	100a.	0 - 0
OBED STANFORD	Poor Quarter	110a.	0 - 0
GEORGE TAYLOR	none		3 - 4
WALTER TAYLOR	Harmon 25a. Priviledge 131a. Hog Quarter 13a. Lott 10a.	161½a.	2 - 3
STEPHEN TAYLOR	Taylors Priviledge 98 3/4a. Taylors Good Luck 25a. Carlisle 48½a.	172¼a.	3 - 3
JOHN VENABLES	Mill Security 30a.	30a.	1 - 1

By Joseph Cottman, Assessor of the Wicomico District

OWNERS NAME	LAND	TOTAL ACRES	White Inhab. MALE-FEMALE
WILLIAM VENABLES	none		3 - 4
THOMAS WABERTEN	none		1 - 0
WILLIAM WALLER	Erlindy 252a.	252a.	4 - 2
THOMAS WATERS	Last Purchase	300a.	1 - 2
JOSEPH WHALEN JR.	none		2 - 5
THOMAS WHALEN	Bottom of the Neck 105a. Security 17½a.	122½a.	4 - 5
WILLIAM WILLIAMS	Williams Choice 50a. Fishers Manor 110a.	192½a.	3 - 4
ISAAC WHITE	none		1 - 4
SAMUEL WILLIAMS	Manor 70a. Bowmans Choice 50a.110a.		3 - 3
PRISCILLA WHITE	widow of M. Bettys Choice	50a.	1 - 2
WILLIAM WINDER JR.	Sandy Plains	686a.	6 - 2
MATTHEW WESTMAN	Poor Quarter	88½a.	2 - 3
BENJAMIN WRILEY	Mill Security ½a.	½a.	2 - 3
JAMES WILLIN	none		1 - 3
ISAIAH WRIGHT	Coxes Fork	80a.	3 - 3
WILLIAM WINDER SR.	Pembertons good will	130a.	0 - 0
JOSEPH COTTMAN	Cottman's Point 50a. Cottmans Freehold 74a. Tanton Dean	310a.	2 - 5

NANTICOKE DISTRICT

OWNERS NAME	LAND	TOTAL ACRES	White Inhab. MALE-FEMALE
ELIZABETH ATKINSON	Atkinson's Venture 155a. Shiles Folly, Hogyard 20a. Fathers Purchase 100a. Mount Alexander 105a. Addn. to Pickle Hot 8½a. Wrights Choice 50a. Small Choice 5a.	557½a.	4 - 2
LITTLETON AIRES	Shiles Folly 40a. Daniels Hope 42½a. MoorFields 456a.	538½a.	4 - 7
RICHARD ACWORTH	Salop 1a.	1a.	1 - 0
GEORGE AIRES	none		0 - 0
SARAH BRINKLEY	none		1 - 2
WILLIAM BRINKLY	Bewdly 33½a.	33½a.	1 - 0
ISAAC BARTLEY	Ware 23½a.	23½a.	2 - 2
ABRAHAM BARTLEY	none		2 - 3
HENRY BARTLEY	Standway 40a. St. Albans 20a. Fair Meadow	219a.	5 - 3
ANN BARTLEY	Stanaway 67½a. St. Albans 3a.	70½a.	0 - 0
JOSEPH BARTLEY	Stanaway	62a.	3 - 3
WILLIAM BENSTON	none		3 - 5
WILLIAM BOUNDS	Addnition to Chance 191½a. Last Choice 70a. Paris 46¼a. Years Land 75a. Shadwell 124a.	395 ¾a.	5 - 4
JAMES BEARD	Hard Fortune 30a. Addn. to Chance 46a. Cordrays Beginning 100a. Long Acre 200a.	376a.	3 - 2
GEORGE BALLARD	none		1 - 4
HENRY CORDRAY	Turnstile	70a.	5 - 2
ROBERT COLLIER JR.	Mt. Hope 45a. Colliers Enlargment 18a. Daughtys Misfortune	67½a.	1 - 0
PHILLIP COVINGTON	Betts Gift 387a. Betts Priviledge 50a.	437a.	3 - 2

By Joseph Cottman, Assessor of the Nanticoke District

OWNERS NAME	LAND	TOTAL ACRES	WHITE INHAB. MALE-FEMALE
NANCY COLLIER	none		0 - 0
ANN COLLIER	Cannons Lot 50a. Georges Priviledge 13½a. Last Choice	113½a.	2 - 1
JOHN CROCKETT	Might have had more	100a.	5 - 2
JOHN S. CONWAY	Finis 58a. Point Marsh 4½a.	62½a.	6 - 1
MATTHEW CANNON	Daniels Adventure 20a. Depford 610a.	630a.	3 - 5
ROBERT COLLIER SR.	chance 21a. Josephs Lott 12a. Bettys Chance 100a. Addition to Chance 42a. Misfortune 21a.	196a.	2 - 3
NICHOLAS E. COLLIER	Last Choice 33a. Can't Tell	124a.	2 - 4
WILLIAM CULLEN	none		2 - 2
ANN DASHIELL	none		1 - 2
JOHN DOUGLAS	Wrights Venture 52½a. End of Strife 9a. Shiles Folly 25a. Shiles Meadow 50a. Clear of Cannon Shot	195½a.	2 - 7
JOHN DASHIELL of Wm.	Dashiells Addn. 102a. Wolf Trap Ridge 50a. Discovery 12a. Chance 4a. Shiles Folly 20a.	188a.	2 - 1
JOHN DORITHY	Disheroons Fancy 25a. Priviledge 30a. Addnition to Your Luck ? 37a.	101a.	6 - 4
RICHARD DUNN	Shadwells late Discovery 20a. Shadwell 100a.	120a.	3 - 4
LEVI DICKERSON	Hopkins Gift 140a. Townsends Situation 53a. St. Albans 60a. Addition 205a.	558a.	4 - 5
JANE DASHIELL	Shiles Folly 65a. Buckingham 50a. Come by Chance 4a. unreadable 33a.	150a.	6 - 6
PRISCILLA DASHIELL	none		0 - 1
MARY DASHIELL	Buckingham 100a. Head Tyaskin 67a. Come by Chance 8a. Shiels Folly 128a.	303a.	0 - 0
JOHN DASHIELL	none		2 - 1
SUSANNAH DASHIELL	Shields Folly 16a. Meeches right 100a. Meeches Desert 66a. Discovery 100a.	282a	1 - 2
JAMES DASHIELL	Shiles Folly 32½a. Meeches Desert 131a. Discovery 100a. Meeches Right 200a.	566½a.	3 - 5
JOSEPH DASHIELL Jr.	none		0 - 0
JOSEPH DASHIELL Sr.	End of Strife 6½a. Last Choice 13a. Meeches Hope 2a. Rich Swamp 135a. Dashiells Addn. 23a.	179½a.	3 - 5
GEORGE DASHIELL	Meeches Hope or Rich Swamp 115a. Come by Chance 22½a. Dashiells Folly 16a. Sherredons Desire 20a. name unknown 16a.	281½a.	2 - 4
RICHARDSON DONOHO	Richardsons Luck	72½a.	2 - 2
WILLIAM DONOHO	Anything 68½a. End of Strife 32a. Nothing 1½a. Little 32½a. Little Hope 27a. name unknown 33a.	197a.	4 - 2

By Joseph Cottman, assessor of the Nanticoke District

OWNERS NAME	LAND	TOTAL ACRES	White Inhab. MALE-FEMALE
WILLIAM F. DASHIELL	Long Hill 150a.	150a.	4 - 1
WILLIAM DASHIELL Sr.	Ventures Priviledge 62½a. Dasheills Purchase 408a.	560½a.	5 - 4
GEORGE DEAN	none		2 - 3
MITCHELL DASHIELL	Recovery 167a. Wolf Pit Ridge 50a. Ventures Priviledge 62½a.	279½a.	2 - 8
THOMAS DASHIELL	none		1 - 1
ISAAC DORITY	none		3 - 2
ARTHUR DENWOOD	Phillips Invention 210a. Georges Meadow 20a. Small Addition 31a.	225½a.	3 - 2
ROBERT DASHIELL	Johnsons Addition 274a. Greenwich 50a. name unknown	417a.	1 - 4
JOHN EVANS Sr.	Evans Second Chance 540½a. Moorsfield 54a.	594½a.	2 - 0
ISRAEL ELLENSWORTH	none		2 - 2
JOHN EVANS of John	Whittys Contrivance	50a.	0 - 0
WILLIAM ELLENSWORTH	Bettys Enlargement 115a. Fishermans Quarter 16a. Beards Adventure 25a.	155a.	3 - 3
JOHN EVANS of Nich°,	Gillis 22a. Finis 181½a. Dormans Improvement 40a. Timber Grove 152½a. Rice Land 320a. Fox Hall 50a. Troy 30a.	656a.	3 - 2
PETER ?FURBUSH	none		1 - 1
MARY BUSKEY FLUELLIN	none		0 - 0
RICHARD FLUELLIN	none		0 - 0
JANE FLEULLIN	none		1 - 6
SAMUEL FLUELLIN	Milk Maid 50a. Prickles Hot Shott 1a. Security 50a. Wolf Quarter 50a. Cannons Choice 5a.	156a.	2 - 2
CHARLES FULLERTON	none		4 - 2
ABENDEGNO GREEN	Fleullins Settlemnet 137a. Addn. to Cow Ridge 237½a. Addition to Ditto, Fleullens Purchase 50a. Ticknell 50a. Security 50a. Wolf Quarter 50a. Cannons Lott 100a. Milkmaid 50a.	1041¼a.	4 - 4
PHILLIP GRAHAM	Westlockneck 300a.	300a.	4 - 2
WILLIAM GILES	none		2 - 2
ELIZABETH GALE	Gales Purchase 606a. Venison pasture 506a.	1202a.	2 - 4
LEVIN GOSLEE	Tullocks Grange 137½a.	137½a.	1 - 0
GEORGE GALE of Levin-	Might have had more 200a. Sidney 16a. Timber Grove 20a. Akam 543a. Troy 20a.	799a.	0 - 0
PATIENCE GAME	none		0 - 0
NANCY HANDY	none		0 - 0
ELIZABETH HANDY	Handys Discovery 270a. Handys Choice 34a. Fleullins Neglect 507½a.		3 - 3
BETTY HANDY	Come by Chance 50a. Doughty Lott 26¼a. Paris 46a. Shadwell 24a. Turnstile 36¼a. Doubtys Misfortune	221½a.	1 - 3

by Joseph Cottman, assessor of Nanticoke District

OWNERS NAME	LAND	TOTAL ACRES	White Inhab. MALE-FEMALE
JOHN HUGHES	Evans Purchase	46a.	2 - 4
KEZIAH HARRIS	Evans Purchase	92a.	1 - 4
DAVID HOPKINS	Ware	70a.	1 - 1
ROBERT HOPKINS	Ware 65a. Samuels Lott 130a.	195a.	6 - 2
NELLY HOPKINS	Ware 10a. Samuels Lott 70a.	80a.	1 - 6
JONATHAN HICKMAN	Fair Meadow 350a. Hickmans Profit 2½a.	352½a.	2 - 3
STEPHEN HOPKINS	Cannons Lott 200a. Hopkins Choice 25a. Sunken Ground	246a.	2 - 2
STEPHEN HICKMAN	none		1 - 3
SARAH HOPKINS	none		0 - 1
ISAAC HOPKINS	Discovery 2½a. Cannons Shott 300a. Hopkins Addition 11½a. Hopkins Last Conclusion 80a.	394a.	2 - 3
GEORGE C. HOPKINS	Georges Pleasure 50a. Chance 2½a. Cannons Shott 100a. Last Choice 50a.	206½a.	6 - 6
WILLIAM HARRIS	none		4 - 4
JAMES HAYNIE	none		0 - 0
THOMAS HOLBROOK	none		2 - 2
JOHN HANDY	Barbers Rest 150a. Daniels Adventure 150a.	300a.	3 - 1
LEVI HOPKINS	none		1 - 2
JOHN HOLBROOK	Sunken Ground 250a. Last Choice 271 3/4a.	521¾a.	2 - 0
ALICE JACKSON	Bewdley 66 3/4a.	66¾a.	5 - 1
JOHN JONES	More Loss than Gain 185a. Addn. to same 53½a.	238½a.	1 - 2
MATHIAS JONES	none		1 - 0
JAMES M. JONES	none		4 - 2
SAMUEL JACKSON	Warrington 35a. Warrington Addition 50a. Chance 77a.	162½a.	2 - 6
GEORGE JAMES	What you please 50a. James Debate 231a. Barbers Addition 50a. Barbers Rest 77a.	408a.	2 - 6
ELIZABETH KING	Mt. Ephraim 900a.	900a.	0 - 3
SAMUEL KING	Kings Misfortune 804a. Mt. Ephraim 467a. Hog Quarter 450a. Fishermans Quarter 130a.	1851a.	0 - 0
SARAH LARRIMORE	Cannons Choice 9¼a.	9¼a.	0 - 2
ELIHU LARAMORE	none		1 - 1
ELIJAH LARAMORE	Recovery	189a.	7 - 3
JOHN LIBBY	Bewdley	35a.	1 - 5
HENRY LOWES	Venture Priviledge 621a. Grandfathers Care 5a. Lowes Chance? 628a.		0 - 0
ISAAC LANDEN	none		4 - 3
CHARLES LEATHERBURY	Small Lott 100a. Warwick 100a. Chance 50a. Leatherburys Fancy 8a. unknown 16a.	273a.	2 - 2
EZEKIEL MATTHEWS	Ware	2½a.	5 - 4
SARAH McCLESTER	Point Marsh	160a.	0 - 0
BETTY McIntire	Williams Lott 20a. Shiles Mistake 30. Daniels Discovery 7a. Safty 9½a. End of Strife 5a. Moorefield 42½a. Dashiells Mistake 8½a. Handys Pasture?, Finish All-	284¼a.	2 - 2

By Joseph Cottman, assoessor of Nanticoke District

OWNERS NAME	land	total acres	White Inhab. MALE-FEMALE
WILLEN McINTIRE	Flowerfield 52a. Daniels Priviledge 35a. Safety 23a. Daniels Chance 30½a. Daniels Hope 37a.	177½a.	2 - 7
JOHN McCLESTER	Woodgate 100a. Sweet Wood Hall 400a. St.Albans 100a.	600a.	1 - 2
BENJAMIN MESSECK	Shadwell	50a.	5 - 5
MARY MESSECK	Ellingsworth Hope	39a.	1 - 3
ELIHU MESSECK	Ellingsworth Hope 50a. End of Strife 100a. Pasturage 224a. Lees Situation 27a. River side Tract 26¼a. Hurry 50a.	378¼a.	3 - 5
JACOB MESSICK	Fellowship 30a. End of Strife 132a. James Lott 17a. Hardy? 50a.	271½a.	4 - 4
RALPH MOOR	Salop 250a. Gillis's Folly	521½a.	1 - 3
JOSHUA E. MOOR	Last Choice 115a. Timber Grove 27a.	142a.	6 - 4
JOHN NORTH	Bewdly	50a.	3 - 4
JOHN NICHOLS	none		2 - 2
HENRY NICHOLS	Ellingsworth Hope 83a. Coffins? Choice 21a. Benjamins Good Sucess 16a.	138a.	2 - 2
HUGH PORTER	Wallaces Centure	45¼a.	7 - 3
WILLIAM PORTER	Hog Quarter	100a.	1 - 0
JOHN PORTER	Whittys Later Invention 200a. Deptford 23½a.	223½a.	2 - 2
WILLIAM POTTER	none		1 - 1
JOHN PARIS	Barren Neck	100a.	1 - 7
GEORGE ROBERTSON	Ignoble Quarter 182a. Mansfield 130½a.	321½a.	5 - 3
DELILAH RICHEY	Mt Hope 105a. Turnstile 5a.	120a.	0 - 2
JOHN ROBERTSON	none		4 - 2
LEVIN RUMBLY	none		2 - 1
SARAH ROBERTSON	none		3 - 3
JAMES READ	none		5 - 5
HEZEKIAH READ	Unknown 200a, Hog Quarter 30a. Chance 27a.	277a.	1 - 1
WILSON RIDER	Westlocks Adventure	200a.	1 - 2
CHARLES RIDER	Tullocks Grange 37¼a.	37¼a.	4 - 2
JOHN RIDERS HEIRS	Midfield 135a. Warwick 35a. Leatherburys Fancy 2a.	192a.	3 - 2
JOHN ROBERTSON SR.	None		4 - 5
PRICE RUSSELL	Trullocks Grange 75a. Meadow 20a. Russells Liberty 173a. Luck 5a. Partnership 15a. Georges Meadow 20a.	205a.	3 - 3
ALEXANDER ROBERTSON	Akam	878½a.	7 - 3
HENRY SELBY	none		2 - 2
THOMAS STEVENS	Bewdly 20a. Late Discovery	70a.	1 - 3
JOHN STERLING	Adams Choice 20a. Adventure 100a. Point Marsh 40a.	160a.	2 - 2
MARY SMITH	Adams Choice 160a.	160a.	1 - 2
WILLIAM STEWART	Brothers Care 131a. Anything 1a. Friends Luck 44½a.	171½a.	3 - 5
JOHN STEWART	Long Hill 150a.	150a.	3 - 2
JOHN SKILLEY	none		2 - 3

By Joseph Cottman assessor of the Nanticoke District

OWNERS NAME	LAND	TOTAL ACRES	White Inhab. MALE-FEMALE
CHARLES SURMAN	Ralphs Venture 100a. Gales Purchase 17a. Good Sucess	167a.	1 - 3
GEORGE D. SCOTT	Sunken Ground 363 Trouble	401a.	2 - 2
GEORGE D. SCOTT	(exec. to Mary Caldwell)none		0 - 0
SAMUEL TOWNSEND	Townsends Situation 203a. St. Albins 20a.	223a.	2 - 2
STEPHEN TULLY	None		2 - 3
CANNON WINRIGHT	Noble Quarter	100a.	5 - 5
EVANS WINRIGHT	Noble Quarter	100a.	2 - 7
JOHN WILLEN	Ignoble Quarter	50a.	3 - 3
SAMUEL WILLEN	Ignoble Quarter 50a. Hickory	126a.	2 - 2
GEORGE WILLIN	Hog Yard 22 3/4a. Hog Quarter 23 3/4a.		5 - 3
LEVIN WILLIN	Hog Yard 21a. Hog Quarter 25a.	44a.	2 - 6
ROBERT WILLIN	Hog Quarter 9½a. Security 17½a. Daniels Choice 39½a. Daniels Priviledge 23a. Union 31½a.	136½a.	5 - 2
WILLIAM WINRIGHT	Addition to Pricklecockholt 136½a. Woolhope 55a.	191½a.	2 - 1
JAMES WALLER	Collins Enlargement 180a. Georges Purchase 24¼a.	24¼a.	1 - 1
JAMES WINRIGHT	Turnstile 95a. Winrights Choice 25a. Fluellins Pleasure 30a. Pasture 130a.	280a.	2 - 3
SOLOMON WINRIGHT	Cannon Shott 100a. Turnsale 6a. Shadwell 12a. Paris 46½a. Hap at a Venture 25a.	190a.	4 - 5
JAMES Willin	Turnstile 70a.	70a.	4 - 4
JAMES WINSOR	New Castle 105a. Old Castle	155a.	4 - 3
LEVIN WALLER	Bewdly 250a. Beards Adventure	275a.	4 - 4
WILLIAM WALLER	Shadwells Choice 281a. Williams Venture 240a.	630a.	6 - 4
ROBERT WALTER Sr.	Wallers Chance 40a. Roberts Lott 15a. Butterfly 5a. Poor Chance 40a.	100a.	1 - 2
JOSEPH WALES	Daniels Mistake rectified 207a. JOsephs Priviledge 195a.	402a.	3 - 2
BETTY WALES	Daniels Mistake Recitified	201a.	1 - 3

REWASTICO DISTRICT

OWNERS NAME	LAND	TOTAL ACRES	White Inhab. MALE-FEMALE
HENRY ACWORTH	Killams Lott 56a.(resurv.from Weatherlys Discovery) Colins Mistake 17½a. Friends Discovery 300a.	373½a.	1 - 5
SARAH ACWORTH	Acworths Purchase 200a. Piney Island 19a.	219a.	1 - 1
WILLIAM ALPHA	none		4 - 2
JOSEPH ALPHA	Acworths Delight 89a. Hendersons Choice 33a.	122a.	2 - 3
TRAIN ACWORTH	United States 273a.(resurv. from Marsh Point) The Ridges 40a. Acworths Delight 60a. Addition 116a. Hogquarter 40a. Discovery 75a. Acworhts Choice 30a.		

By John Weatherly assessor of REWASTICO DISTRICT

OWNERS NAME	LAND	TOTAL ACRES	White Inhab. MALE-FEMALE
TRAIN ACWORTH	Luck by Chance 100a. Marsh 15a. Weatherlys Addition 85a.	833a.	3 - 4
RICHARD ACWORTH	Hog Quarter 30a. Acworths Delight 100a. The Ridges 10a.	140a.	3 - 0
BENJAMIN ADKINSON	Greens Luck 230a.(resurv. of Marys Choice) Last Conclusion 182 3/4a.(resurv.of Commons) Atkinsons Grief 15a. Small Lot 8½a. Acworths Delight 68a. Addition 30a. Choice 202a.	714a.	2 - 2
JOHN ANDERSON	Greens Luck 88a. Friends Discovery 20a. Greens recantation 176a. Chance 100a. Quakeson 65a. Andersons Addition 3½a. Andersons Chance 3½a.	456a.	6 - 3
WILLIAM ADKINSON	none		2 - 5
JAMES ANDERSON	Warrenton 88a. Egypt 12a.	100a.	2 - 2
EDWARD AUSTON	none		1 - 2
GEORGE ANDERSON	none		2 - 1
WM.DAVIS ALLEN	Gillis's Adventure	100a.	0 - 0
JOHN ACWORTH	none		1 - 0
WILLIAM ARMSTRONG	none		2 - 3
ROBERT ANDERSON	Newhaven	100a.	3 - 3
MARGARET ANDERSON	Come by Chance,Longton 47a.	67a.	2 - 2
STEPHEN ADAMS	Come by Chance 70a.	70a.	0 - 0
MARGARET BOTHAM	none		3 - 3
THOMAS BEDSWORTH	Parramores Pasture 48a. Largee & Akalow 87¼a. Addition 50a.	185½a.	2 - 3
ELIZABETH BROWN	Wilsons Mistake	200a.	5 - 4
JOHN BENNETT	First Choice	50a.	4 - 3
LITTLETON BENNETT	Bennetts Venture	50a.	1 - 2
JESSEE BIRD	Venture 50a. Hackley 117a.	167a.	3 - 3
PRISCILLA BANKS	Kings might 12a. Adams Discovery 32½a. Halls Adventure 168a.	202½a.	0 - 1
JAMES BENNETT	Handys Purchase 200a. Spences Choice 125a.	325a.	1 - 1
ROBERT BROWN	Browns Beginning 269¼(resurv. of Which you please) Browns beginning 27a. Partners Choice 22a. Browns __ Bye 16 1/3a.	67 1/3a.	3 - 2
DEEN BADLEY	Gladstens Adventure 64a. Deens Chance 5a. Hardshift 11a.	80a.	5 - 5
CHARLES BADLEY	Hardshift	75a.	3 - 2
ELIZABETH BADLEY	Tower Hill resurvey 24a. Tower Hill 11 1/3a. Chance 8½a. Royal Exchange 143a.	186⅝a.	2 - 3
EZEKIEL BELL	Mount Suzzy	57⅞a.	4 - 6
JAMES BADLEY Sr.	Addn. to Collins Adventure	104a.	2 - 4
BENJAMIN BIRD	New Haven 208a. Denwoods Den	258a.	5 - 5
RACHEL CARMICHAEL	Lott 2a. Roads Misfortune 10a. Warrenton 190a.	202a.	0 - 3

By John Weatherly, assessor of the REWASTICO District

OWNERS NAME	LAND	TOTAL ACRES	White Inhab. MALE-FEMALE
DOUTY COLLIER	Egypt & Garham	62½a.	1 - 3
NICHOLAS CANTWELL	Weatherlies Adventure	100a.	5 - 1
JOHN COLLINS	Purchase 269½a. Lone Tree Island 374a.	643½a.	0 - 0
AHAB COSTON	none		3 - 4
DANIEL CORDRY	Quierson Neck	50a.	2 - 3
JOHN COOPER	Hard Fortune (resurvey)	224a.	4 - 3
ABRAHAM COOPER	Addition 50a.(resurv.Bedford) Bedford 83a.	133a.	2 - 3
SAMUEL COOPER	Bedford	70a.	1 - 0
THOMAS CORDRY	Wilsons Discovery	75a.	4 - 6
THOMAS CONNERLY	Irelands eye 150a. Venture	200a.	4 - 5
NATHAN CULVER	United States 200a. Point Patience & Mill Lot 26a. Peace and Quiet 167a.	563a.	1 - 1
THOMAS COOPER	Bedford 83a. Addition 50a.	133a.	1 - 3
ESME BAILY	Black Water 25a. The Worst is past 132½a. The Deers Lott & Supply 329a.(resurv.of Conclusion) Whetstone 200a. High Suffolk 50a. Addition to Flower Field 379a.	975½a.	5 - 5
WILLIAM DORMAN	none		2 - 2
MATTHEW DORMAN	Weatherlys Purchase 250a. Pasturage 60a. Trains Lott 80a. Addition 30a. Compleat 25a. Purchase 16a. Killems Lott 125a. (resurv.of Weatherlys Discovery)	586a.	7 - 7
ARTHUR DASHIELL	Late at Noon 50a. Wainstock 5a. End of Strife 40 1/3a. Dashiells Chance 184a. Last Choice 64½a. Late at night 50a. Come by Chance 24a. Largee 116a. Dashiells Sucess 159 1/3a. =	607⅓a.	7 - 2
GEORGE DASHIELL	Good Luck	3⅛a.	5 - 2
LEVI DASHIELL	First Choice 110a. Chance 90a.	190a.	2 - 2
JOHN DORMAN	Morris Lott	43a.	1 - 2
CHARLES DAVIS	Woodfield	100a.	2 - 2
WILLIAM DORMAN Sr.	Partners Choice	150a.	4 - 3
Capt.JOSIAH DASHIELL	none		0 - 0
JOSEPH DUNN	Jonathans Prospect	75a.	2 - 2
DANIEL DARBY	Redburn	140a.	1 - 4
BENJAMIN DARBY	Catchelors Choice	22½a.	3 - 2
LEVI DEEN	Deens Venture	182½a.	1 - 2
JAMES DEEN	Deans Lott 10a. Deans Chance 10a. Royal Exchange 90a.	110a.	3 - 2
SARAH DARBY	Batchelors Choice 50a. Darbys Addition 146a. Williams Adventure 36a.	333a.	0 - 3
DAVID DUTTON	Poor Chance 41a. Crooked Chance 50a.	91a.	1 - 2
CHARLES DASHIELL	Donnigal 130a. Buck Hill 37a. Mount Charles 66a.	233a.	7 - 1

By John Weatherly, assessor of the REWASTICO District

OWNERS NAME	LAND	TOTAL ACRES	White Inhab. MALE-FEMALE
ISAAC DASHIELL	Ellis's Addition	70a.	3 - 2
JOSEPH ELLIS Sr.	Ellis's Addition 96a. (resurv.of Quiet Entrance)	96a.	4 - 4
EDWARD ELLIS	Covingtons Choice	109½a.	4 - 4
LEVIN FOLLIN	Woodyard	155a.	2 - 3
ESTHER FLETCHER	Caseway	153½a.	0 - 1
THOMAS FLETCHER	Caseway	153½a.	1 - 1
ELIZABETH FLETCHER	Little Holsey 200a. Betsys First Choice 200a.	400a.	1 - 5
JOHN FOWLER	Addition	52a.	3 - 0
DANIEL FRAZIER	none		4 - 3
LEVIN FLETCHER	Wolfs Pitt Hill 42a. Crooked Chance 133a.	175a.	5 - 3
JAMES FLETCHER	Nicholsons Settlement 140a. Saw Mill Supply 16a.	156a.	5 - 6
GEORGE FLETCHER	Casoway	170a.	1 - 5
JACOB GIBSON	none		1 - 2
JOSEPH GILLIS	Maidens Lott 100a. Chestnut Ridge 18a. Gillis's Addn 18a.	136a.	5 - 5
JOHN BRUMBLE	Acworths Delight 93a. Daniels Discovery 8a.	100a.	4 - 5
WILLIAM GILLIS	Oak Hall 960a. Friendship	985a.	0 - 0
THOMAS GILLIS	Maiden Lott 100a. Gillis's Venture 5a.	105a.	2 - 3
THOMAS GLASTER	Maidens Lott 100a	100a.	3 - 2
ANNE GUPTON	Casoway 43½a. Woodfield 56a. New Addition 18a.	117½a.	2 - 5
HENRY GALE	Chelson 125a. Monmouth 73a. _____amton 112a.	310a.	1 - 0
ISAAC GILES	Partners Choice 50 1/3a. Giles Lott 250a.	300⅓a.	3 - 6
WILLIAM GODDARD	Partners Choice 100a. Collins Folly 72a. Ill Wind 33¼a.	205¼a.	2 - 3
JAMES GOSLEE	none		6 - 1
LEVIN GALE	none		0 - 0
LOUDER GRAVENOR	Best Leg	100a.	1 - 0
MARY GRAVENOR	Best Leg	50a.	0 - 3
EZEKIEL GRAHAM	Quankeson Neck 50a. Ezekiels Conveniency 20a.	70a.	3 - 3
SAMUEL GAME	Covingtons Choice	55 a.	2 - 0
JEREMIAH GAME	Covingtons Choice	60a.	1 - 0
SAMUEL GREEN	none		6 - 5
EUNICE GILES	Partners Choice 50a. Giles Lott 175a.	225a.	2 - 1
JAMES GUNBY	Marys Venture	20a.	0 - 0
ABIHU HARRIS	Largee 38 1/3a.	38 1/3a.	2 - 2
JOHN HARDY	Killams Lott	45a.	3 - 2
BEAUCHAMP HULL	HOG QUARTER 130a. Acworths Deligt 36a. Woodyard 40a. Pharsalia 91a. Western Fields	411a.	4 - 3
BENJAMIN GRAHAM	Quakenson Neck 50a. Marys Venture 20a.	70a.	1 - 0
LEVI HARRISON	none		7 - 1

By John Weatherly, assessor of the REWASTICO District

OWNERS NAME	LAND	TOTAL ACRES	White Inhab. MALE-FEMALE
ISAAC HENRY	Woodfields 119a. Last Choice 8 3/4a. Pharsalia 91a. Western Fields 150a.	$368\tfrac{3}{4}$a.	2 - 2
GILLIS HOWARD	First Choice	150a.	1 - 1
MARY HARRIS	Acworths Delight 75a. The Ridges 25a.	100a.	0 - 0
JOHN HOPKINS	Chelsey 100a. Gillis's Adventure 150a.	250a.	2 - 3
ALLEN HOWARD	Partners Choice	100a.	3 - 3
JOHN HOBBS	Greens Luck 2¼a. Greens recantation 10a.	12½a.	2 - 2
PHILLIS HUMPHREY	Venture 50a. Fork of the Branch 9a. Keens Lott 50a. Green Hill 8½a.	117½a.	1 - 2
JOSEPH HUMPHREY	Keens Lott 100a. Green Hill 16a. Fork of the Branch 9a.	122a.	2 - 2
JOSHUA HUMPHREY	Keens Lott 100a. Green Hill	175a.	4 - 2
LEVIN HANDY	Lott 200a. Balanan 363½a.	563½a.	2 - 2
HENRY HANDY	Pemberton 350a. Surveyors Mistake 15a. Friends Choice 10a. Shiles Folly 15a. Maiden Head	690a.	3 - 4
WILLIAM HORSEY	Sankeys Island 33 2/3a. Weatherlys Marshes 45 1/3a. Fathers Care 200a. Glasgow Green 25¼a. Pinney Tree Island 13 2/3a. Chance 6 1/3a.	$673\tfrac{11}{12}$a.	5 - 2
ISAAC HANDY	Handys Care 41a. Chance 1¼a. Cork land 100a.	105¼a.	1 - 1
WILLIAM HANDY Sr.	Pemberton 270a. High Suffolk 220a. Shiles Folly 15a.	405a.	1 - 1
BETTY HANDY	Handys Neck 793a. Shiels Folly 808a.		1 - 5
SAMUEL HOWARD	Ellis's Frolick 50a. Nelms Difficulty 55a.	171a.	6 - 2
JOSHUA HITCH	High Suffolk 260a. Hitches Discovery 30a. Wilsons Discovery 100a. Fathers Neglect 100a. Last Choice 80a. Maddux's Luck 229a. Flowerfield 333a.	1021a.	5 - 6
LEVIN HARDY	none		2 - 2
MARY HOWARD	none		1 - 3
SARAH HITCH	High Suffolk 391a. Come by Chance 566a.		1 - 6
THOMAS HITCH Jr.	High Suffolk 224a. Fathers Delight 16a.	240a.	1 - 0
WILLIAM HARRIS	Purchase 16a. Largee 62 1/3a.	78 1/3a.	1 - 1
ISAAC HORSEY	Cherry Tree Island 13 2/3a. Chance 6 2/3a. Sankeys Island 33 1/3a. Weatherlys Marsh 5 1/3a.	59a.	0 - 0
CHARLES HENDERSON	none		1 - 3
JOSEPH HUST	Ill Neighborhood	50a.	1 - 1

By John Weatherly, assessor of the REWASTICO District

OWNERS NAME	LAND	TOTAL ACRES	White Inhab. MALE-FEMALE
LEVIN HUFFINGTON	Lazy Hill 85½a. Hard Fortune 50a.	135½a.	1 - 1
ANGELO HUFFINGTON	Batchelors Folly	234a.	4 - 4
LAZARUS HUFFINTON	Batchelors Folly 125a. Royal Exchange 100a.	225a.	1 - 2
THOMAS HUMPHREYS	Say Mill Supply 110a. James Fortune 15a. Blade Side 50a.	165a.	3 - 4
JUDITH HAYNIE	The Victory of Wisdom over Haynies adversary	287½a.	2 - 4
JOHN HENRY	Spring Hill 1000a. Greens Loss 75a. Harsh Meadow 320a. New Addition 71a.	1460a.	2 - 4
THOMAS HITCH Sr.	Denwoods Den 98½a. Peace of quietness 36a.	135¼a.	3 - 2
JAMES HAYNIE	Victory of wisdom over Haynies Adversary	155a.	0 - 0
ELIJAH HEARN	Stanes 525½a. Support 95a. Sand Hill 20a. Addition to Stanes 37a.	677½a.	2 - 2
BENJAMIN HEARN	Saw Mill Supply	55a.	2 - 2
THOMAS HEARN	Sandy Hill 75a. Gravelly Hill 50a.	125a.	0 - 0
LOUDY HITCH	Ellis's Addition 20a.	20a.	4 - 2
ELIAS HITCH	Denwoods Den 117½a. Hot Hill 30a. Hitchens Chance 22a.	169½a.	2 - 4
JOSHUA HASTINGS	Hazzard	36a.	0 - 0
JOSHUA HUFFINGTON	Youngs Purchase 150a. Hard Fortune 37½a.	187½a.	1 - 0
RICHARD HAYNIE	Victory of Wisdom over Haynies Adversary 100a. Friends Assistance 300a. Ill Neighborhood	850a.	1 - 0
EZEKIEL HITCH	Hitches Choice	50a.	3 - 1
ANN HUFFINGTON	Neighbor Vezation 155a. Ezekiels Conveniency 20a.	175a.	1 - 1
JAMES HUST	Ill Neighborhood	100a.	2 - 2
THOMAS HUFFINGTON	Bacons Folly 25a. Forked Malberry 20a. Havannah 20a.	65a.	1 - 4
JONATHAN HUFFINGTON	Barren Quarter 15a. Hard fortune 37½a.	52½a.	3 - 2
ESTHER JONES	Pharsalia 275a. Good Luck	307a.	2 - 4
WILLIAM JOHNSON	Friends Choice 106a. Good Luck 32a. Friends Choice 124a. Elgates Lott 50a.	312a.	1 - 0
ELIJAH JOHNSON	Hackley 50a. Mulberry Landing 3a.	53a.	1 - 1
JOANNA JOHNSON	none		0 - 1
LEVIN IRVING	Charlestown 50 3/4a. Last Choice 30 3/4a. Security 2a. First Choice 36 1/3a. False Dispute 22a.	139¼a.	2 - 3
RICHARD JAMES	Batchelors Folly	204a.	4 - 2
JONATHAN JACKSON	none		3 - 2
JOHN JOHNSON	Saw Mill Supply	40a.	2 - 1
EDWARD KILLUM	Killums Lott	230a.	3 - 4

By John Weatherly, assessor of the REWASTICO DISTRICT

OWNERS NAME	LAND	TOTAL ACRES	White inhab. MALE-FEMALE
EVERTON KENNERLY	St.Giles 190a. First Choice 10a.	200a.	5 - 1
WILLIAM KENNERLY	Acworths Delight 100a. Wilsons Discovery 75a.	175a.	2 - 5
WILLIAM KERSEY	none		1 - 5
SAMUEL KING	Furniss Chance 231a. Gethsemene 300a. Delight 256a. Long Delay 174a. Clover Field 534a. Slipe 25a. Nutters Adventure 468a. Pastuarage 45a. Recovery 3½a. Addition 50a. Nutters Adventure 50a. Addtion to Nutters Contrivance 311 3/4a. Bottom of the Neck 153a. Priviledge 76a.	2367¼a.	1 - 2
MATTHEW KEMP	Chelsea 90a. Monmouth 75a.	165a.	2 - 3
LEVIN KING	Balaam	280a.	0 - 0
JOHN LANKFORD	Killums Lott 36a.(resurvey)	36a.	2 - 4
WILLIAM LLOYD Jr.	Lott 108½a. Norths Den 40a. Dear Park 36a. Davis Pasture 25a. Round the Clock 31a.		
WILLIAM LLOYD Jr.	Foes Confusion 60a. Trial Lott 4½a. Denstons Lott	304½a.	4 - 3
WILLIAM LLOYD Sr.	Savanah Lott 15a. Killums Lott 22a.	37a.	3 - 4
ARTHUR LANDEN	none		1 - 2
JOHN LANGSDALE	Woodstock 95a. End of Strife 151 3/4a.	246¾a.	4 - 3
JOHN LEATHERBURY Sr.	Egypt 32a. Fairham 55a. Fitch field 100a. Fairfield 15a. Little Bit 14a.	216a.	2 - 4
JOHN LEATHERBURY Jr.	Old Berry	400a.	1 - 1
CANNON LANK	Eversham	150a.	2 - 2
NATHAN LOW	Weatherlys Adventure	164a.	3 - 3
BENJAMIN LANKFORD	Cubys Chance 100a. Saw Mill Supply 50a. Wilsons Good Luck 19½a.	169½a.	3 - 1
JAMES LLOYD	none		1 - 0
JOHN LORD	Tower Hill	67a.	2 - 2
MARY LANKFORD	Cubys Chance and Saw Mill Supply	40a.	3 - 5
HUDSON LOWE	Addition to Collins Lott	194a.	4 - 6
THOMAS LEATHERBURY	none		2 - 2
THOMAS LANK	Addition to Collins Lott	100a.	3 - 4
BENJAMIN MESSECK	none		6 - 2
ANDREW MURPHY	none		1 - 3
EBE MORRIS	Partners Choice	100a.	1 - 2
WILLIAM MOORE Jr.	Moor's Adventure	27½a.	2 - 2
MARY MOOR	Turkey Cock Hill	100a.	6 - 2
WM. MOOR s/o Wm.	Woodyard 85a. Fitchfield 15a.	100a.	2 - 4
WILLIAM MOORE Sr.	Turkey Cock Hill 50a. Woodyard 200a. Cains Creek Mill	270a.	1 - 1
JAMES MOOR	Fitchfield 30a. Farham 15a. Woodyard 55a.	195a.	4 - 3

By John Weatherly, Assessor of the REWASTICO District

OWNERS NAME	LAND	TOTAL ACRES	White Inhab. MALE-FEMALE
WILLIAM McBRYDE	Nithsdale 289a. Vulcans Vineyard 29a. Cherry Tree Island 13 2/3a. Weatherlys Marshes 45 1/3a. Sankeys Island 33 1/3a. Chance 6 2/3a.	417a.	2 - 0
WILLIAM McCLEMMY	Newhaven 207a. Maidens Fancy 50a. Last Discovery 22½a. Addition 7a. Confusion 27½a.	314a.	1 - 1
ELIZABETH MADDOX	none		1 - 1
ELIZABETH McLALLY	Partners Choice 80a.	80a.	5 - 2
JOSEPH MELSON	Friendship 79½a	79½a.	2 - 4
ELLENDER McCLANEN	Western Fields 50a. St.Giles	100a.	3 - 5
JAMES McDANIEL	Bedford 134½a. McDaniels Luck	184½a.	2 - 2
WILLIAM McDANIEL	none		1 - 1
BETTY MARTIN	Poor Chance 36a. Small Hope 14a.	50a.	3 - 4
WILLIAM MILLS	BetsHannah 90a. Honest Purchase	193½a.	4 - 7
WILLIAM MARIEN	Wheel of Fortune	150a.	1 - 0
ISAAC MOORE Sr.	Addn. to Collins Adventure	150a.	2 - 2
ELIJAH MOORE	Hazzard	25a.	2 - 1
BETTY MADDUX Jr.	Covingtons Choice	47½a.	2 - 1
JOHN MADDUX	Covingtons Choice 35a. Whitefield 130a. Peace and Quietness 15a.	180a.	4 - 1
ISAAC MADDOX	Whitefield	130a.	7 - 4
BENJAMIN McCLELLAN	Humphreys Chance 100a. Saw Mill Supply 55a. Piney Grove	199a.	2 - 2
JOHN McCLESTER	White Chappel	300a.	0 - 0
ROGER NICHOLSON	Chance 100a.	100a.	2 - 1
HUETT NUTTER	Givans Security	100a.	1 - 3
JAMES NELSON	Monmouth 100a. Largee 72¼a.	172¼a.	2 - 2
BENJAMIN NELSON	Huffingtons Venture	100a.	4 - 2
JAMES NIGHT	none		2 - 1
WILLIAM NUTTER Sr.	Delight 127¼a. Middle Tract 100a. Morris Lott 110a. Marsh Ground 100a. Contention 37½a. Nutters Adventure 232a. Dormans Delight 50a. Kingston 100a. Handys Care 37a. Ross 30a.	1003¾a.	6 - 2
JOHN NELSON Sr.	Chelsea 28½a. Egypt 68a. Stephenson 100a. Harris Small Lott 52½a. Huffingtons Venture 60a. Largee & Akalow 72¼a. Fairham 182a.	443¼a.	3 - 3
JOSHUA NICHOLSON	Saw Mill Supply	50a.	2 - 1
JOSEPH NICHOLSON	Williams Green 50a. White Glade 50a.	100a.	2 - 3
CHARLES NICHOLSON	Nicholsons Lott 100a. Peace and Quietness 9½a.	109½a.	5 - 5
JAMES PHILLIPS	Lyons Folly 150a. Wales 50a. Weatherlys Reserve 32a. Maidnes Choice 25a. Kellams Lott 38a. Givans Discovery 50a.	345a.	7 - 7

By John Weatherly, Assessor of the REWASTICO District

OWNERS NAME	LAND	TOTAL ACRES	White Inhab. MALE-FEMALE
JAMES PARRAMORE	Purchase 50a. Weatherlys Purchase 18	68a.	1 - 0
McKIMMA PORTER	Fathers Delight 100a. Acworths Contrivance 13 1/3a. Last Choice 62a. Porters Meadow 17½a	192$\frac{5}{6}$a.	1 - 2
GEORGE PHILLIPS	Casoway 109a. Woodfield 107a.	216a.	3 - 3
JOSEPH PIPER	Cloverfield 66 1/3a. Heedless Cost 150a. Wilten 100a. Marsh Hook 75a. Once Again 75a.	466$\frac{1}{3}$	1 - 0
AGNES PIPER	Cloverfield 33 1/3a. Salisbury Plains 200a.	233$\frac{1}{3}$	0 - 4
JOSIAH PHILLIPS	None		4 - 2
JESSEE PARAMORE	Wilsons Discovery	149¼a.	2 - 3
DANIEL PHILLIPS	Spanish Oak Ridge 100a.	100a.	8 - 4
JAMES PRITCHET	Venture 35½a. Snows Hill 75a. Last Choice 32½a. Victory over wisdom of Haynies Discovery	213$\frac{3}{4}$a.	4 - 3
JOSIAH & GILLIS POLK	Pasturage 50a. Corkland 16a.	66a.	1 - 0
JOHN PHILLIPS	Ill Neighborhood 118a. Friends Folly 230a.	348a.	6 - 3
JACOB QUINTON	Wilsons Discovery	100a.	1 - 2
THOMAS RUSSELL	Shantavannah 42a. Largee & Akelow 87½a.	129½a.	6 - 3
JACOB RHOADS	Warrington 10a. Daniels Discovery 16a. Shantavannah 158a. Hendersons Choice 32a. Den Pasture 75a.	251a.	4 - 3
ISAAC RHOADS	End of Strife	40a.	4 - 3
SARAH RUSSELL	none		0 - 3
CORNELIUS REEDY	Largee & Athalow	72¼a.	3 - 3
WILLIAM RENCHER	Morris Lott 140a.	223a.	1 - 3
FISHER ROBERTS	Pharsalia 30a. Flower Fields 165a. Elgate Lott 25a. Tasmania 75a.	315a.	4 - 2
LEME RECORDS	Morris Lot	183a.	4 - 6
ARCHELAS RECORDS	Partners choice 100a. Good Luck 77a. Addition to Whetstone 183a. Foxshall 28a.	388a.	1 - 2
PRICE RUSSELL	Partnership 15a.	15a.	0 - 0
JOHN ROBERTSON Sr.	Long Delay 100a. Venture 50a. White Hall 50a. Tower Hill 229a.	429a.	4 - 4
WILLIAM ROSE	Wheel of Fortune	50a.	3 - 5
JOSEPH ROLES(heirs)	Gladsteens Adventure & Gladsteens Choice	100a.	0 - 0
JOHN RUMMER	Pig Pen	50a.	4 - 1
JAMES ROBERTSON	Tower Hill 55½a. Peter 50a. Goodness going over 13a.	118½a.	2 - 2
MARY ROBERTSON	none		1 - 2
ISAAC ROBERTSON	none		2 - 1
JOHN ROBERTSON Jr.	Ireland Eye 150a. Small spot of Ground 10a. Dispute 92a. Royal Exchange 113a.	366a.	3 - 2

By John Weatherly, Assessor of the REWASTICO District

OWNERS NAME	LAND	TOTAL ACRES	White Inhab. MALE-FEMALE
STEPHEN STEVENS	Piney Island 8a. Acworths Purchase 100a.	108a.	4 - 3
AARON STERLING	Killams Discovery 132a. Woodyard 35a. Batchellors Purchase 50a. Susage 5a. Chance 100a. Friendship 25a.	347a.	3 - 2
JAMES SMITH	Morris Lott 200a.	200a.	2 - 2
WILLIAM STANFORD	Newberry	297a.	2 - 2
THOMAS STANFORD	Little Nelsey	100a.	2 - 2
MARGARET STEVENS	Little Nelsey	100a.	0 - 2
WILLIAM STONE	High Suffolk 310a. Gillis's Addition 100a. Maddox Lott 37a. Handys Pasture 14a.	462a.	3 - 4
JOHN SMITH	High Suffolk & Come by Chance 100a. Elgates Lott 25a. Tasmania 75a.	200a.	2 - 2
JOHN STARLING	none		0 - 0
ABRAHAM SMITH	Quienson Neck 100a. Hard Fortune 50a.	150a.	4 - 2
LEVIN SMITH	Friends Folly 50a.	50a.	1 - 0
PETER SIMPSON	Three Brothers	130a.	3 - 4
DRUMMON SIMPSON	Greens Loss	75a.	4 - 3
ROBERT SCROGIN	Hazzard 9½a. Cottmans Adventure 317a.	326½a.	1 - 3
JOHN SCROGIN	Fairfields 170a. Anything 100a. Addktion to Anything 50a. Fairfields Addn. 47½a.	376½a.	6 - 3
JOSEPH SCROGIN	Stains 130½a. Hazzard 33½a.	164a.	1 - 1
GEORGE TWILLEY	Woodstock 20a. Chance 100a.	120a.	8 - 5
RICHARD SEBREN	none		3 - 4
WILLIAM TAYLOR Sr.	Weatherlys Contrivance	150a.	2 - 3
WILLIAM TAYLOR Jr.	none		1 - 0
EZEKIEL TAYLOR	First Choice	100a.	1 - 0
JAMES TRAIN	Slipe 25a. Weatherlys Purchase 302a.	327a.	1 - 0
JOHN THORNS	Piney Island	132½a.	4 - 4
WILLIAM TURPIN	Marshhook 25a. Once Again 25a. Weatherlys Purchase 113a. Shiles Lott 10a. Orphans Lott 39a. Partnership? 7a.	219a.	2 - 2
JOSEPH TWILLEY	none		2 - 1
HENRY TRAYDER	Maddux Luck	147a.	4 - 6
GEORGE TULL	Good Luck 130a. Venture 23a.	153a.	
JOSHUA TURPIN	none		5 - 2
JAMES TULLY	Bedford	18a.	4 - 5
JOSHUA TAYLOR	none		2 - 1
JAMES TAYLOR	Taylors Addition 117½a. Taylors Interest 50a.	167½a.	4 - 2
JACOB TAYLOR	none		3 - 1
THOMAS TAYLOR	none		1 - 3
RICHARD TRAYDER	Chance 50a. Last Choice 25a. Come by Chance 134a.	209a.	1 - 1
WILLAIM TAYLOR (Broad Creek)	Folly	25a.	3 - 3

By John Weatherly, assessor of the REWASTICO DISTRICT

OWNERS NAME	LAND	TOTAL ACRES	White Inhab. Male-Female
ABRAHAM TAYLOR	Taylors Addition 117a. Tower Hill 55a. Gladsteens Choice & Adventure 100a.	272a.	5 - 6
ISAAC TAYLORS heirs	Taylors Addition 142a. Tower Hill 305½a.	447½a.	0 - 0
BARTHOLOMEW TAYLOR	Taylors Chance	100a.	1 - 0
RACHEL VENABLES	Western Fields 300a. Partners 380a.		5 - 3
CHARLES VAUGHN	Scotts Chance	160a.	4 - 3
ELIJAH VINSON	Snow Hill 55a. Bally Berger 180a. Caldwells Chance 27a. Point Patience & Mill Lott 112a.	384a.	4 - 3
ISAAC VINSON	Corkland 100a. Denwoods Den 229½a. Piney Hill 23a.	352½a.	3 - 2
GEORGE VINSON	New Carrey 50a. Last Chance	159¼a.	4 - 2
BENJAMIN VENABLES	Western Fields	600a.	4 - 7
JOSEPH VENABLES	Troublesome 100a. Flat Glade 100a. Warehouse Island 4a. Algate 150a. Wilsons Lott 200a. Mills End 406a. Browns Priviledge 33½a. Western Fields 300a. Horse Island 16½a. Venables Pretentions 60a. McLollys Folly 12a. Tremone? 10a.	1392¼a.	4 - 3
GABRIEL WALTER	none		1 - 1
JOHN VICASS	Wilsons Discovery	100a.	1 - 1
JOHN WALLER	Weatherlys Ridges	100a.	6 - 3
JAMES WEST	Acworths Delight 75a. The Ridges 25a.	100a.	2 - 4
CONSTANTINE WEATHERLY	Weatherlys Ridges 100a. Acworths Folly 10a. Calder	180a.	2 - 3
EPHRAIM WILSON	Darby	100a.	3 - 1
JAMES WILSON	Darby	109a.	5 - 5
JESSEE WEATHERLY	Weatherlys Lott 75a. Partnership 55a.	130a.	2 - 5
JAMES WEATHERLY	Partnership 93½a. Acworths Contrivance 35a. Prevention 58a. Acworths Folly	313½a.	1 - 2
WILLIAM WINDER	Farringtons Purchase 261a. Weatherlys Find 10a. Commons 117a. Twillys Ridge 134a. Addition 50a. Last Choice 86a. Partnership 228a. Prevention 12a. Acworths Contrivance 33a. Lions Lot 96½a. Sons Choice 50a. Washington 130a.	1412½a.	3 - 3
WILLIAM WHITTINGTON	Givans Security 200a. Lions Lot 8a.	208a.	2 - 1
JOHN WATERS	Dormans Delight 250a. Shiles Choice 220a. Jones Chance 100a. Tubmans Lott 37 1/3a. Quantico 27a. Densons? Chance 60a.	694⅓a.	3 - 4
JOHN WEATHERLY	Partnership 151a. Parsenham 70a. Acworths Folly 158a. Casoway 50a. Chance 21a. Good Luck 121a.	392½a.	4 - 4

By John Weatherly assessor of the REWASTICO District

OWNERS NAME	LAND	TOTAL ACRES	White Inhab. MALE-FEMALE
GEORGE WILSON Sr.	Lankfords Delight 42¼a. Purchase 45a. Casoway 300a. Wilsons Good Luck 16a. Wilsons Meadow 3a.	412¼a.	3 - 1
GEORGE WAGGAMAN	Calcutta 505a. Vulcans Vineyard 100a.	605a.	0 - 0
MARY WILLIAMS	Luck by Chance 60a. Ebbys Frolick 10a.	70a.	1 - 3
JOHN WILSON	Darby	100a.	1 - 2
AILCE WRIGHT	Queisons Neck	180a.	0 - 2
GEORGE WILSON	none		1 - 2
HANDY WRIGHT	none		1 - 2
ELIZABETH WRIGHT	Solomons Delight	100a.	1 - 4
HENRY WALKER	Walkers Folly 30a. Deans Folly 200a.	230a.	5 - 3
SOLOMON WRIGHT	none		2 - 2
JOSHUA WRIGHT	none		2 - 2
JACOB WRIGHT	Chance 50a. Now or Never 53½	103½a.	3 - 6
JOHN WALES	Golds Delight 200a. Tit for Tat 15a. Giles Lott 123a.	338a.	5 - 1
THOMAS WALLER	Eagletown 100a. York 50a. Wallers Fancy 100a. Victory over wisdom of Haynies Adversary 50a.	338a.	3 - 3
EBENEZER WALLER	Cow Lott 330a. Peace & Quietness 20a. Mill Lot 2a. Wallers Meadow 20a. Mill Support 37a.	409a.	3 - 5
RICHARD WALLER	Victory of Wisdom over Haynies Adversary	59a.	0 - 0
GEORGE WALES	Golds Delight 200a. Tit for Tat 15a.		4 - 0
CHARLES WEATHERLY	Ill Neighboorhood 200a. Friends Folly 174a.	374a.	5 - 4
STEPHEN WRIGHT	Friends Folly	150a.	4 - 2
JOHN ANSLEY	Quieson Neck	50a.	1 - 2
WILLIAM HICKS	Neighbors Vexation	140a.	0 - 0
WILLIAM TULLY	Betsys Estate	50a.	0 - 0

PRINCESS ANNE DISTRICT - Monie 100

OWNERS NAME	LAND	TOTAL ACRES	White Inhab. MALE-FEMALE
THOMAS AKEMAN	Addition to Littleworth 8a. Addition to Littleworth 13½a. Wrights Folly 41. Contention & Discovery 26½a.		
LLOYD ABBIT	none		1 - 3
WILLIAM ABBIT	none		3 - 4
JOHN ABBIT	Ballahack 200a. Forlorn Hope 100a. Polks Folly 100a. Clonwell 100a. Forlorn Hope Addn. 70a. Whittys Lott 50a. Come at last 10a.	570a.	2 - 2

By Thomas Irving, assessor of the Princess Anne District- Monie 100

OWNERS NAME	LAND	TOTAL ACRES	White Inhab. Male-FEMALE
GEORGE AUSTIN	Addition to Whittys Lot	20a.	2 - 4
JOSEPH AUSTIN	none		2 - 7
GEORGE ABBOTT	Intent Contention	47a.	2 - 2
JOHN ADDAMS Sr.	Good Luck	27a.	0 - 0
ALEXANDER ADAMS(Heirs)	Survey	50a.	0 - 0
ISAAC BOZMAN	More and Case it	130a.	2 - 5
WILLIAM BELL	More & Case it 432a. Bozmans Addition 52a.	484a.	1 - 3
GEORGE BALLARD	Covingtons Meadow	100a.	0 - 0
ELIAS BALEY	none		2 - 1
WILLIAM BALLARD(of Arnold)	none		2 - 3
SARAH BALLARD	Almodington	250a.	4 - 3
JARVIS BALLARD	Almodington	50a.	2 - 2
ARNOLD BALLARD Sr.	Sucess	121a.	1 - 6
NEHEMIAH BOZMANS(heirs)	Prospect	449a.	0 - 0
ARNOLD BALLARD(Monie)	Covingtons Meadow 3a. Sassafras Neck 67a. Jones Choice 75a.	161a.	4 - 2
MARY BALLARD	none		0 - 3
THOMAS BOZMAN	none		4 - 5
MARY COVINGTON	Carnys Chance 46 3/4a. Adventure 16 3/4a.	63½a.	1 - 1
LEVIN COVINGTON	none		1 - 1
JOHN CAVANAUGH	Nicholsons Adventure & Little worth 55a. Addn. to Little Worth 18a.	73a.	2 - 4
ROBERT CAVANAUGH	Intent Contention	75a.	1 - 0
JAMES CAMBALL	Belfast 25a. St. Peters Neck 88a. Chance 2½a.	115½a.	3 - 1
JOSEPH CANTWELL	none		1 - 2
MARY DAUGHTY	none		0 - 3
LEVIN DASHIELL	Mitchels Improvement 250a. Jones's Choice 175a. Mitchells Choice 250a.	675a.	1 - 3
JOHN DASHIELL	none		3 - 5
JOHN DAVIS	none		3 - 2
JOSHUA DENNIS	none		2 - 3
JESSE EVANS	none		3 - 5
WILLIAM EVANS	none		3 - 1
WILLIAM ELZEY	Almodington	340a.	1 - 0
ARNOLD ELZEY	Almadington & Support	1242a.	1 - 0
ROBERT ELZEYS(Heirs)	Somethingworth	68a.	0 - 0
ANN ELZEY	none		0 - 1
CHARLES GATES	Brownstone	102a.	3 - 2
LEVIN GALE Jr.	Addition	500a.	1 - 4
JOSEPH GILLIS	none		2 - 2
WILLIAM GILLIS	More and Case it	158a.	1 - 0
LEVIN GALE	Bare Swamp 7a. Priviledge 7a. Carneys Chance 164a. Addition 1130a. Covingtons Conclusion 348a. Covingtons Adventure 60a. Sweetwood 200a. Stoney Ridge 300a. Priviledge 14 3/4a. Piney Grove 21¼a.	=2252a.	6 - 3

By Thomas Irving, assessor of the Princess Anne District- Monie 100

OWNERS NAME	LAND	TOTAL ACRES	White Inhab. MALE-FEMALE
EZEKIEL GILLIS	Colebrook	200a.	0 - 0
MATHIAS HOBBS	Good Luck 91 1/3a. Hobbs Conclusion 211¼a. Carneys Chance 46 3/4a.	349⅓a.	6 - 2
ANN GIBSON	none		0 - 2
WILLIAM HATH	none		2 - 5
LAMBERT HYLAND	St. Peters Neck	517a.	3 - 2
WILLIAM HAYWARD	Pasturage	387a.	0 - 0
JAMES HOPKINS	none		4 - 5
JOHN HOPKINS	none		2 - 5
MOSES HORNER	none		3 - 3
DOLLY HALL	Golden Quarter 53a. Long Delay 53a.	106a.	1 - 4
WILLIAM JONES Sr. (Gr. Monie)	Jenkins Mistake 165a. Mannings Resolution 250a.	415a.	2 - 3
GEORGE JONES (Gr.Monie)	none		2 - 2
MARY JONES Sr.	none		1 - 2
HENRY JACKSON	Bozmans Adventure & Robins Adventure 110½a. More & Case it 221a. Bozmans Adventure 45a. Robins Addition 27a.	403½a.	0 - 0
DANIEL JONES	Mannings Resolution	397a.	2 - 1
WILLIAM JONES(of Thomas)	Jones Choice	150a.	2 - 1
ROBERT JONES	Long Delay 12¼a. Jones Priviledge 80a. Jones Addition 100a. Golden Quarter & Long Delay 55a. Lums Increase 7½a.	254¾a.	5 - 1
ANN JONES	Golden Quarter & Long Delay	100a.	0 - 1
MARY JONES(of Thomas)	none		0 - 1
PHILLIP JONES	Jones Purchase	107a.	2 - 5
JAMES JONES	none		1 - 0
JOHN JONES(Goose Ck)	Bozmans Advent & Robertsons Addition 110½a.	110½a.	5 - 5
SARAH JONES	none		0 - 1
JOHN JONES (of Mary)	none		2 - 4
JOHN JONES (for (Thomas Jones Heirs)	Comforts Adventure 28a. Covingtons Meadow 7a. Sassafras Neck 137a.	172a.	0 - 0
LEWIS JONES	Laytons Convience 70a. Lums Amendment 161a. Jones Chance	426a.	1 - 0
JOHN JONES(Dames Quarter)	Laytons 130a. Gravesend 150a. Windsors Prevention 30a. Purgatory 19a. Jones Adventure 50a. Lums Amendment 161a.	806½a.	4 - 2
LEWIS JONES	The Downs	100a.	
GEORGE JONES(Dames Quarter)	none		1 - 0
JOHN JONES(Little Monie)	Jones Choice	350a.	6 - 2
CHARLES JARVIS	None		1 - 0
WILLIAM KING	none		5 - 2
JAMES KILLEY	none		0 - 0
NEHEMIAH KING	Barbadoes 300a. Piney Island 10a. Cross 36½a. South Foreland 37½a.	374a.	0 - 0
JOHN LOKIE	none		3 - 1

By Thomas Irving, assessor of the PRINCESS ANNE District-Monie 100

OWNERS NAME	LAND	TOTAL ACRES	White Inhab. MALE-FEMALE
JOHN LAWES (Devils Island)	LAWS ADDITION 25a. Greenwich toa. North Foreland 300a. Laws Defence 90a. Self Possession 29a.	505a.	5 - 1
JOHN LAWES (Hune Point)	Laws Addition	36a.	3 - 1
JOLLY LEATHERBURY	Covingtons Vineyard	300a.	1 - 0
WILLIAM LAWES	Littleworth 50a. Something worth 50a. Pt. Panthers Den 96a. Happy Addition 42a.	238a.	2 - 2
JOHN LAWES (Monie)	Somethingworth	66½a.	1 - 2
WHITTY McCLEMMY	Colebrook 350a. Something-worth 68½a.	418½a.	2 - 3
JAMES MARTIN	none		7 - 2
JAMES MACOMB	none		2 - 1
OWEN McGRATH	none		3 - 4
JOHN MACOMB	Hackley & Jessamin	165a.	4 - 3
JOSEPH McVEY	Newmans Last Conclusion	10a.	3 - 2
JOHN McGRATH	Owens Improvement 150a. Delight 100a. Middle 52a. Davids Chance 38a. Refuge 50a. Hobs Adventure 150a. Priviledge 35a.	525a.	4 - 2
JOHN MARTIN	Keep Poor Hall	100a.	4 - 5
HENRY MUIR	none		4 - 4
THOMAS MARTIN	none		2 - 4
ROBERT MARTIN	none		1 - 2
HENRY WALSTON MILES	Myrtle Swamp 100a. Strife 38 3/4a. James Content 84a. Wrights Folly 17a.	293¾	3 - 5
GEORGE MILES	Addition to Littleworth 100a. Addition to Littleworth 14a. New Virginia 60a.	174a.	1 - 1
THOMAS MACOMB	none		2 - 2
THOMAS MILLS	none		2 - 2
WILLIAM McDORMAN	none		3 - 2
THOMAS NOBLE	Addition	3¼a.	0 - 0
AILCE NEWMAN	Newmans Last Conclusion	219a.	0 - 1
THOMAS NEWMAN	Newmans Last Conclusion	488a.	5 - 4
JOSIAH NIGHT	none		2 - 2
SAMUEL OWENS	none		2 - 3
ELIZABETH PARKER	Mannings Resolution	133a.	0 - 2
GEORGE PHOEBUS Sr.	Jones Adventure 50a. Addition to Jones Adventure	55a.	1 - 2
JOHN PHOEBUS Jr.	Nicholsons Adventure 6a. Littleworth 49a.	55a.	5 - 5
JOHN PHOEBUS Sr.	Nicholsons Adventure 97a. Brothers Agreement 79a. Littleworth 27 & 16a.	219a.	5 - 2
WILLIAM PHEBUS	none		1 - 0
HENRY PHEBUS	none		1 - 0
SAMUEL PHEBUS	Littleworth 94½a. Nicholsons Adventure 41a. Addition to Littleworth 120a.	255½a.	1 - 2
JOAB PARKES	Gunners Range 64a. Contention	110a.	1 - 1

By Thomas Irving, assessor of PRINCESS ANNE District -Monie 100

OWNERS NAME	LAND	TOTAL ACRES	White Inhab. MALE-FEMALE
THOMAS ROBERTS	Covingtons Meadow and Covingtons Adventure	202a.	2 - 0
BARTLETT ROBERTS	Edwards Lott 50a. Jesamine 50a. Bought of Wallaces Heirs 106a.	206a.	1 - 0
JOSEPH REED	Addition to Littleworth	69½a.?	3 - 0
JOHN ROBERTS	Edwards Lott	50a.	2 - 0
WILLIAM ROBERTS	Elliotts Chance 69a. Edwards Chance 100a. Edwards Lott 113a. Davids Destiny 150a. Williams Beginning 50a. Jesamine 48a. Polks Meadow 200a. Venture Priviledge 100a. Roberts Recovery 59a. Green Pasture 200a.	1087a.	2 - 1
ELEANER ROBERTS	none		0 - 1
SARAH ROBERTS	none		0 - 1
MARTHA ROBERTS	none		0 - 1
NICHOLAS ROE	Purgatory	37½a.	3 - 5
RICHARD ROE	none		2 - 1
MARY SKIRVING	Owens Choice 172½a. no name 57a. Borwns Lott 168½a.	398a.	0 - 1
THOMAS SWIFT	none		1 - 1
SMITH SIMS	Satisfaction	116a.	3 - 5
WILLIAM STEWART	none		2 - 5
JOSHUA SMITH Jr.	none		3 - 1
BENJAMIN SASSER Jr.	Mill Point	18½a.	1 - 0
JAMES SPICER	White Oak Swamp 100a. James Content 42a.	142a.	1 - 1
WILLIAM SASSER Sr.	Rowdee 200a. Newport Panell 50a. Somethingworth 150a. Sassers Folly 100a. Addition 50a. Sassers Lott 50a. Wolf Harbour 50a. Hanslop 50a.	800a.	3 - 4
WILLIAM SHELTON	none		3 - 3
BENJAMIN SASSER Sr.	Somethingworth 134a. Panthers Den 192½a. Happy Addition 65a.	411a.	1 - 2
MARY SMITH	St. Peters Neck Georges Adventure, Chance & Belfast 87½a.	115½a.	0 - 2
THOMAS SLOSS	Sucess 300a. Marlborough 130a. Rainsborough170a. Bloyses Hope 100a. Conclusion 176a. Pennywise 50. Pennywise 30a.	756a.	3 - 3
THOMAS SHORES	none		3 - 1
MICHAEL TIMMONS	None		2 - 6
LEVIN WILSON	Bozmans Addition 148a. Happy Addition 100a. Glasgow 275a. Wilsons Discovery 75a. Kilgland 350a. Security 75a. Tilbury 75a.	=1098a.	0 - 0
WILLIAM WAGGAMAN	Long Meadow 78a. Davids Chance 250a. Adventure 200a. Davids Amendment 37a.	565a.	1 - 0

By Thomas Irving, assessor of PRINCESS ANNE District-Monie 100

OWNERS NAME	LAND	TOTAL ACRES	White Inhab. MALE-FEMALE
PHILLIP WINGATE	none		4 - 3
THOMAS WHITNEY	Whitneys delight 132a. Mungars Choice 82a.	214a.	7 - 8
WILLIAM WHITNEY	none		1 - 6
GOWAN WRIGHT	Rainsborough 30a. Chance 51a. Marlborough 20a. Bloyces Hope 30a. Wrights Folly 62 3/4a. Contention 50a. Intent 167a. Wolfs Harbour 41¼a.	449a.	1 - 9
JOHN WEBSTER	none		4 - 1
JAMES WILSON	Weatherlys Chance 20a. Brownstone 300a. Denwoods Inclusion 21a. Wilsons Addition 50a. James Wilderness 39½a. Wilsons Conclusion 318a.	748a.	1 - 0
DENWOOD WILSON	Wilsons Conclusion 1001a. Kilgland 250a. Security 75a. Tilbury 25a. Wilsons Discovery 25a. Glasgow 75a. Improvement 57a. Wilsons Addn. 31 3/4a. Small Addition 3 3/4a.	1533½a.	3 - 4
SAMUEL WILKINS	Haywards Purchase 456½a. Turkey Ridge 100a. Addition 24a. Dormans Addition 97½a. name unknown 17a. Woolf Den 9a. Dormans Conclusion 54a. Dormans Folly 103 3/4a.	753¾a.	3 - 4
LEVIN WOOLFORD	Woolford 900a. Happy Addition 100a. Wolfords Adventure 50a. Meadows 80a. Locust Hammock 25a. Part of front to Locust Hammock 37½a. Webley 250a. Hamiltons Fortune 8¼a.	1430¾a.	6 - 5
JOHN WRIGHT	Worst is Past 150a. Long Lott 50a. Friends Advice 40a.	240a.	3 - 2
ANN WALLER	Locust Hammock 25a. Front to Locust Hammock 37a. Wallers Adventure 300a. Friends Chance 45a.	407a.	1 - 1
JOHN WHITE Jr.	Friends Content 27a. Oxford 100a. Father & Sons Desire 39a.	166a.	4 - 4
JOHN WINDSOR (for Frank Roberts heirs)	Elliotts Choice 100a. Roberts Adventure 10a. Edwards Lott & Jesamine 30a.	140a.	4 - 4
HENRY WALSTON	none		4 - 5
WILLIAM WHITE	none		3 - 1
MARY & MARGARET WALLACE	Friends Acceptance 25a. Father and Sons Desire 121½a. Dames Quarter 40a.	186½a.	0 - 2
FRANCES WHITE	James Delight 100a. Outlett 100a.	200a.	3 - 4
THOMAS WHITE	Friends Content and Father and sons Desire	92a.	6 - 5

By Thomas Irving Assessor of Monie 100

OWNERS NAME	LAND	TOTAL ACRES	White Inhab. MALE-FEMALE
CHARLES WILLIAMS	Charles Adventure 140a. Harrison? Lott 264a	404a.	2 - 6
ELIZABETH WILLIAMS	Roberts Lott	100a.	0 - 1
HENRY WAGGAMEN	Cumberland 40a. Good Luck 91 3/4a. Carnys Chance 103a. Waggamens Purchase 947a. Vulcans Vineyard 100a. Carneys Chance 100a.	1482¾a.	2 - 1
DAVID WALLACE	Winders prevention	30a.	3 - 3
LAZARUS WINDSOR	none		4 - 3
RICHARD WALLACE	Long Delay 90a. Woolwick	240a.	4 - 4
JABEZ WEBSTER	none		1 - 1
JOHN WINDSOR Jr.	none		2 - 2
MESHACK WEBSTER	none		2 - 2
THOMAS IRVING	Malcombs Lott 400a. Habnob 216a. Goerges Adventure 986a. Cow Quarter 100a. Daniels Adventure 150a. Warwick & Midfield 100a. Line House 25½a.	1985½a.	3 - 4

By Thomas Irving Assessor of MANOKIN 100a.

BALLARD BOZMAN	Double Purchase 500a. Double Purchase 107¼a.	607¼a.	1 - 1
CHARLES BANNISTERS Heirs	Double Purchase	160a.	0 - 1
PHILLIP BARCABUS	Double Purchase	25a.	2 - 4
MITCHELL BANNESTERS heirs	Double Purchase	80a.	0 - 0
REBECCA BENSTON	Woolover 100a. Buck Ridge	131½a.	0 - 0
Rev. HAMILTON BELL Sr.	Hamiltons Fortune 873 3/4a. Waltons Improvement 55½a. Davis Choice 12a. Clover Fields 113 3/4a. Parkers Delight 4a.	273a.	1 - 0
Rev. HAMILTON BELL Jr.	none		3 - 2
DAVID BROWN	Browns Chance	113a.	0 - 0
THOMAS BLAKE	none		3 - 3
WILLIAM BALLARD	Derry 77a. Smiths Resolve 100a. Goldsmiths Delight 100a. Ballard & Kings Lott 48a.	325a.	1 - 2
JOSHUA BOSTON	Brothers Agreement	200a.	4 - 2
ANDREW F. CHANEY	Nutters Purchase 8½a. Friendship 179a. Nutters Purchase 70½a. Haywards Purchase 5a.	262½a.	5 - 5
WILLIAM CARROL	Chance	90a.	3 - 4
GEORGE CORBIN	Cow Quarter 62a. Double Purchase 401a.	463a.	0 - 0
JOHN DONE	Dones Nest Egg	555½a.	2 - 4
ISAIAH DORMAN	Dormans Conclusion 17a. Dormans Discovery 131a.	148a.	2 - 2
ELIZABETH DORMAN	Dormans Discovery & Golden Quarter	32½a.	0 - 1

By Thomas Irving, Assessor of MANOKIN 100a.

OWNERS NAME	LAND	TOTAL ACRES	White Inhab MALE-FEMALE
CHASE DORMAN	Dormans Discovery 40a. Nelsons Choice 55a.	95a.	4 - 4
WILLIAM DREDDEN	none		0 - 0
MARY DENSTON	Chance 66a. First Choice	84a.	3 - 3
LEAH DIES	none		0 - 1
JOSHUA DAVIS	none		3 - 2
JOHN DURHAM	none		4 - 2
JAMES ELZEY	Double Purchase	200a.	1 - 3
GRACE FURNIS	Amity 97¼a. Pools Hope 100a. Fair Spring 100a. Great Hope 6½a.	285½a.	2 - 2
WILLIAM FURNISS	Double Purchase	165¼a.	1 - 0
THOMAS FURNISS	Fair Spring 200a. Great Hope 13½a.	213½a.	0 - 0
GEORGE FOURTON	none		1 - 0
JOHN GRAY	none		2 - 2
THOMAS GIVANS Jr.	Hopewell 150a. Thomas's chance 91a.	241a.	4 - 4
THOMAS GIVANS Sr.	Grandfathers Gift 100a. Low Land 50½a.	150½a.	5 - 3
JOHN GIVANS Sr.	Lowland 45a. Giddens Luck 34 3/4a. Hopewell 140a. Givens Chance 74a. Hog yard 22¼a. Tilghmans Adventure 7½a. Givans Last Choice 3a.	382¾a.	1 - 5
WILLIAM GIVANS Sr.	Tilghmans Luck 30a. Good Luck 5 3/4a. Hopewell 10½a. Tilghmans Venture 47a. Pools Hope 60a.	153¼a.	2 - 4
EZEKIEL GILLIS	(for James Robertsons Heirs) Glanville Lott	436a.	2 - 3
WILLIAM HATH	Wansbury 50a. Wilsons First 2½a. Hoggridge 30a. Haths Chance 141½a. Strife 1½a. Myrtle Swamp 45a. Hogyard 4½a. Hog Ridge 25a.	200a.	3 - 8
REVEL HORSEY	Double Purchase 300a. Hopkins Destiny 50a. Partners Desire	490a.	3 - 5
MARGARET HAILES	Margarets Purchase	15a.	0 - 1
WILSON HATH	Wilsons First 97¼a. Hog Ridge 53a. Spittle 22a. Luck Still	369¼a.	
ISAAC HOLLAND	Smiths Recovery	99a.	1 - 0
JOHN JONES(Manokin)	Moorsburrough	309a.	4 - 3
WILLIAM JONES(Manokin)	Winter Quarter 255 3/4a. Bridgets Lott 370a. Friends Advice 356a.	981a.	2 - 2
JOHN IRVING	Sarahs Joy & Double Purchase	200a.	1 - 0
ZOROBABEL KING	Clover Fields 92a. Baltimore 68¼a. Kings Glade 324a.	484¼a.	1 - 1
MARY KING(Jesse Kings Heirs)	Oxhead	230a.	0 - 3
JESSEE KING	Turpins Choice	100a.	1 - 0
LEVIN KING(ofNehemiah)	Double Purchase 293a. Addn. to Double Purchase 30a. Come by Chance 250a. Double Purchase 60a. 30a.	633a.	0 - 1

By Thomas Irving, assessor of MANOKIN 100a.

OWNERS NAME	LAND	TOTAL ACRES	White Inhab MALE-FEMALE
NEHEMIAH KING	Kingsland 300a. Partners Choice 797½a. Dublin Kings Chance 163 Free Purchase 100a. Welcome 50a. Double Purchase 200a. Kings Choice 75a.	1595½a.	2 - 0
FRANCES KING	Bowerly	500a.	0 - 2
SAMUEL KILLUM	Hannah's Delight and Exchange	200a.	4 - 4
Rev.JACOB KERR	Daughters Dower and Bannisters land	225a.	2 - 3
LEVIN KING(of Zorobable)	none		1 - 0
LEVIN LANKFORD	Labour	117a.	4 - 3
LITTLETON LANDEN	none		3 - 3
JOHN LAYFIELD	none		2 - 3
SOLOMON LONG	Amity 247a. Bearsley 16 3/4a.	263¾a.	5 - 4
DAVID LONGS Heirs	Amity 2 3/4a. no name 9a.	11	0 - 0
EPHRAIM LANKFORD	Welcome	180a.	2 - 6
JOHN LAWES	Hartlebury 100a. Resurvey Hartlebury 104 3/4a. Addition 74a. name unknown 25a.	203¾a.	1 - 3
MATHIAS MILES	Fair Meadow 24a. Georges Fortune 8a. Desert 100a. Fair Meadow 196a. Mills Chance 23a. Meadowland 120a. Bare Ridge 172a. Knavery Discovered 145a. Friends Advice 123a. Colrain 50a. Comesly Chance 45a. Good Luck 50a.	996a.	3 - 4
ELIZABETH MILES	Conclusion	138a.	0 - 2
SAMUEL MURRAY	none		1 - 3
WILLIAM MATTHIAS	none		3 - 3
THOMAS MITCHELL	none		1 - 3
BRIDGET MITCHELL	Amity	66½a.	1 - 2
WILLIAM MITCHELL	Amity	133½a.	6 - 6
WILLIAM MILES(of Samuel)	land	110a.	4 -4
ISAAC MURRAY	none		4 - 4
GEORGE MITCHELL	none		3 - 3
ISAAC MITCHELL	none		1 - 3
ROBERT MATTHEWS	none		3 - 3
WILLIAM McGRATH	none		1 - 3
SAMUEL MUIR	Double Purchase	100a.	5 - 2
BENJAMIN POLK	Small Addition 6¼a. Smiths Hope 100a. Williams Adventure 64a. Double Purchase 50a. Addition to Smiths Hope 194a.	514¼a.	5 - 5
MARY POLLITTE	Hog Quarter 100a. Last Choice 26¼a.	126¼a.	0 - 1
THOMAS POLLITTE	Wilsons Finding 68a. Pollitts Victory 194a. Wainsbury 50a. Hazzard & Liberty 38a. Little plantation 2 2/3a.	352⅔a.	2 - 4
WILLIAM POLLITTE	Addition 3¼a. Haywards Purchase 113a. Fair Meadow 17a. Last Choice 30a. Liberty 20 3/4a. Geddes Outlett 70a.	154a.	2 - 0

By Thomas Irving, Assessor of MANOKIN 1Q0

OWNERS NAME	LAND	TOTAL ACRES	White Inhab. MALE-FEMALE
BENJAMIN PEWSY	Labour	75a.	3 - 3
WILLIAM POLK (For I. Handys Heirs)	Kings Glade 11¼a. Indian Bones 7½a. Wolf Harbour 150a. Bare Chance 15a. Cloverfields & Indian Bones & Kings Glade 231¼a. Clover Fields 236a. Coney Warren 125a.	575¾	2 - 5
JAMES POLK	Double Purchase 113a. Smiths Hope 236a. Conclusion 85a. Royal Exchange 12½a. Illchester 150a. Addition to Illchester 156a.	752½a.	1 - 0
JOHN PARKER	Davis Choice 179a. Parkers Fortune 20a.	199a.	4 - 6
WILLIAM PRICE	none		2 - 1
JOHN PRICE	none		2 - 1
JOHN ROUNDS	Giddeons Luck & Tilghmans Adventure	120a.	3 - 5
RANDAL REVEL Jr.	Double Purchase	100a.	1 - 1
JAMES RIGGEN	none		3 - 0
ABIGAIL REVEL	none		0 - 2
RANDAL REVEL Sr.	Double Purchase	333½a	3 - 3
WILLIAM SMITHS (Heirs)	none		0 - 0
GEORGE SHIPHAM	none		3 - 4
JOSHUA SMITH	none		1 - 2
JONATHAN STANFORD	Good Luck 50a. Content 30a.	80a.	4 - 1
WILLIAM STEWART	Panthers Den	217a.	5 - 2
WILLIAM STRAWBRIDGE	Widows Chance 1059a. Addition 82a. Conveniency 100a.	1241a.	2 - 2
SAMUEL TAYLOR	Haphazzard	60½a.	1 - 1
JOSHUA TAYLOR	none		2 - 4
ISAIAH TILGHMAN	Arabia 71a. Beaver Dam Branch 66a. Tilghmans Adventure 100a. Amity 196a. Somethingworth 44a. Woolfe Den 49½a. Bears Hall 100a.	586½a.	3 - 4
ABRAHAM TAYLOR	Second Addition 51a. HapHazzard 60½a.	111½a.	4 - 4
JOSEPH TILGHMAN	Pools Hope	51a.	2 - 0
Dr. JOHN WINDER	Nelsons Choice 250½a. Haywards Purchase 121½a. Dormans Addition 69a.	441a.	3 - 0
JAMES WILLIS	none		2 - 2
JESSEE WALSTON	Smiths resolve	100a.	5 - 5
WILLIAM WALTON	Walstons Improvement 150a. Winter Quarter 51 2/4a.	201¾a.	1 - 4
GEORGE WAGGAMEN	Waggamens Lott	359a.	1 - 1
DAVID WILSON	Cloverfield 808½a. Gulletts Advisement 138a.	846½a.	3 - 5
SAMUEL WILSON	Great Hope 700a. Killmania	850a.	2 - 2
JAMES WILSON	Wilsons Purchase 609a. Clanville 4a.	613a.	1 - 0

By Thomas Irving, assessor of PRINCESS ANNE 100

OWNERS NAME	LAND	TOTAL ACRES	White-Inhab MALE-FEMALE
JOHN ANDERSON	Beckford 1 Lott		3 - 8
JOHN BLOODSWORTH	Beckford 2 lots		2 - 4
Dr. ANDREW F. CHANEY	Beckford 2 lots		0 - 0
FREDERICK DIGNER	Beckford 3 lots	2½a.	5 - 5
JOHN DENWOOD	Beckford 1 lot	¼a.	3 - 3
ROBERT ELZEYS (heirs)	Grays Advantage 100a. Manloves Discovery 250a.	360a.	0 - 4
Dr. ARNOLD ELZEY	none		1 - 0
FRANCES GATRO	Beckford	¼a.	0 - 2
LEVIN GALE Esq.	Beckford 3 lots		0 - 0
JOHN HOWARD	Beckford 2 lots		4 - 5
HENRY JACKSON Esq.	Beckford ½ lot & #11. Beckford 470 3/4a. Waggamens Lott 23a.	493¾a.	3 - 4
CHARLES JONES	Beckford 1 lot	3/4a.	2 - 3
THOMAS MADDUX (heirs)	Rowleys Ridge 14a. Beckford 1 lot 3/4a.	14¾a.	0 - 0
ZADOCK LONG	none		1 - 5
SAMUEL McCLEMMY	Beckford 1 lot		1 - 0
ROBERT MONCURS (heirs)	Beckford 3 lots		0 - 0
JOHN PURSE	Beckford 1 lot		1 - 3
WILLIAM POLK (for Is. Handys heirs)	Beckford 2½ lots		0 - 0
THOMAS POLLITE	Beckford 1 lot		0 - 0
STEPHEN SHEPHERD	none		1 - 1
WILLIAM STRAWBRIDGE	Beckford ½ lot		0 - 0
GEORGE WAGGAMEN	Beckford 1 lot		0 - 0
GEORGE WHETHIAR	none		1 - 3
SAMUEL WILSON	Beckford 1 lot		0 - 0
HEBER WHITTINGHAM	Beckford 1 lot		3 - 2
HEBER WHITTINGHAM (for Elijah Tull)	Beckford 1 lot		0 - 0

By Thomas Handy, assessor for Great Annamessex 100

OWNERS NAME	LAND	TOTAL ACRES	White-Inhab MALE-FEMALE
WILLIAM ADDAMS	Industry 75a. HapHazzard 5a.	80a.	1 - 3
PEGGY ADDAMS	Priviledge 75½a. Partners Agreement 200a.	275½a.	2 - 2
?udley ADDAMS	Adams Chance	128a.	1 - 3
LEVI ADDAMS	none		6 - 2
BETTY ADDAMS	none		0 - 1
JOSEPH ARNO	none		5 - 5
CHARLES AVERY	none		1 - 3
SAMUEL BEDSWORTH	Providence 215a. Bedsworths Choice 62½a. Bald Ridge 106a.	383⅓a.	3 - 3
MARY BENSTON	none		0 - 2
RISDON BOZMAN	none		1 - 0
SARAH BEAUCHAMP Jr.	Contention	168a.	0 - 1
DANIEL BEAUCHAMP	none		5 - 4
GEORGE BOZMAN	Colburn	22¼a.	2 - 5

By Thomas Handy, assessor for GREAT ANNAMESSEX 100

OWNERS NAME	LAND	TOTAL ACRES	White Inhab. MALE-FEMALE
JOSEPH BALLARD	Langfords content Enlarged	85a.	2 - 1
JEAN BEAUCHAMP	Contention 45a. Discovery 50a. Remanent 13a. Hartford Broad Oak & Catlins Venture 41a.	149a.	4 - 2
RICHARD BOSTON	LongRidge 40a. Ledbourn 19a. Bostons Lott 43a.	102a.	1 - 1
JOHN BROUGHTON	Longs Chance 110a.	110a.	0 - 0
LEVIN BOSTON	Bostons Lott 37½a. Bostons Choice 102a. Ledbourn & Beauchamp 40a.	179½a.	2 - 3
ISABELLE CONWAY	Ware Point enlarged 50a. Addition 31a. Condockaway 50a. Rambling Point 10a.	141a.	2 - 3
JAMES CURTIS	Armstrongs Lott	311a.	2 - 5
THOMAS COTTINGHAM	Boston 132a. Rumbling Point 5a. Turkey Swamp 10a.	157a.	1 - 5
SAMUEL CURTIS	Three Brothers 200a. Curtis Lott 100a.	300a.	5 - 3
DAVID COTTINGHAM	Turkey Pine 56a. Need 22a. Vulcans Vineyard 35a.	113a.	3 - 4
WILLIAM COTTINGHAM	Boston 24a. Mumford 7a. Chance 63a. Revenge 30a. Williams Lott 60a. Rumbling Point 15a.	214a.	5 - 3
JOSHUA CATLIN	Harford Broad Oak 40 3/4a.		1 - 2
WILLIAM CATLING	Harford Broad Oak 162a. Branfield 16a.	178a.	2 - 0
NATHAN COHOON	Littleworth 53a. Cheesmans Chance 60a. Security 100a.	213a.	1 - 3
THOMAS COTTINGHAM	Chance & Bostons Addition	137¾a.	4 - 1
NEEL COLBERT	None		5 - 1
MARY COLBERT	none		0 - 3
WILLIAM CULLEN Sr.	none		1 - 3
WILLIAM CULLEN Jr.	none		2 - 1
NEHEMIAH CATLIN	none		4 - 4
WILLIAM COLBERTS(heirs)	none		3 - 1
LEAH COHOON	none		0 - 5
THOMAS DIXON Sr.	Dixons Choice Enlarged 216a. Bostontown 30a. Dixons Addition 45a. Lankfords Content Enlarged 12a. Neighbors Content 3¼a. Winter Harbour 30a.	336¼a.	2 - 1
THOMAS DIXON Sr.	Dixons Lott	110a.	
WILLIAM DIXON Jr.	Security 202½a. Dixons Lott	227½a.	2 - 0
AMBROSE DIXON	Security 202½a. Dixons Lott	227½a.	2 - 3
THOMAS DIXON(James)	Second Choice 215a. Dixons Lott 30a.	245a.	1 - 1
THOMAS DAVIS	Discovery 100a. MiddleStrand	185a.	5 - 5
ISAAC DISON SR.	Dixons Choice & Dixons Bull 249a.	259a.	2 - 2
JOSEPH DAWSEY	none		4 - 4

By Thomas Handy, assessor for GREAT ANNAMESSEX 100a.

OWNERS NAME	LAND	TOTAL ACRES	White Inhab MALE-FEMALE
JOHN DOREY	none		1 - 1
PETER DERRICKSON	none		1 - 0
WILLIAM FOUNTAIN	Normandy 261a. Neighbors Agreement 20a. Marsh Ground 120a.	401a.	4 - 3
CHARLES FORD	Promise Land	100a.	6 - 5
JOHN FOUNTAIN	none		1 - 0
STEPHEN GARLAND	Davidges Purchase 335½a. Three Borthers 237½a. Salisbury 50a. Somertshire 13¼a. Garlands Lott 18½a. What you will 7a.	651¾a.	1 - 3
JOHN GIPSON	none		2 - 3
LEONARD GURNEY	none		2 - 2
BETTY GUNBY	none		0 - 2
JOHN HOWARD	North Sampiere	97½a.	0 - 0
SMITH HORSEY's heirs.	Horseys Chance 223a. Horseys Venture 45a. Hazard 106a. Beards Neck 100a.	474a.	0 - 0
MARY HORSEY	Jones Island	470a.	2 - 1
GEORGE HOWARD	Longs Chance 18a. Rain Water 6½a. Buck Ridge 24 3/4a. Priviledge 13½a.	62¾a.	5 - 6
ROBERT HALL	no name(a resurvey)	36a.	3 - 5
ISAAC HANDY	Handys purchase 200a. Marsh land 60a.	260a.	1 - 3
ISAAC HALL	Halls Hammocks 50a. Halls Choice 100a. School House Ridge 50a.	200a.	3 - 3
JOSHUA HALL	Halls Adventure 100a. Halls Hammook 50a.	150a.	3 - 5
CHARLES HALL	Halls Pasture 34a. Halls Kindness 172a.	206a.	5 - 4
ESTHER HALL	Halls Pasture 16a. Halls Kindness 86a.	102a.	0 - 4
ZOROBABEL HALL	Desert 175a. White Oak 49a.	224a.	2 - 5
OUTERBRIDGE HORSEY	Dixons Lott 100a. Colbourn 216a. Horseys Inclusion 544a. Horseys Lot 51a. Dixons Kindness 20½a. Dixons Bull 25a. Horseys Pretension 280¼a. Dixons Choice enlarged 4½a. Mickle meadow 150a. Wards & Horseys Chance 9a.	1119½a.	1 - 5
JOHN HANDY	none		2 - 2
JOHN HALL Jr.	none		2 - 2
WILLIAM HOPEWELL	none		3 - 2
THOMAS HALL	none		3 - 4
SAMUEL HALL	none		5 - 2
JOHN HORSEY(of Smith)	none		1 - 0
WILLIAM HOWARTH	none		2 - 2
THOMAS JONES	Conclusion	17a.	1 - 1
LEVI JOHNSON(mulatto)	Davids Adventure	99a.	3 - 5

By Thomas Handy, assessor of the GREAT ANNAMESSEX 100

OWNERS NAME	LAND	TOTAL ACRES	White Inhab. MALE-FEMALE
BETTY JONES(Cabel's wife)	none		2 - 1
JOHN JONES(Kingstown)	none		4 - 2
ISAAC JOHNSON	none		1 - 2
LEVI JOHNSON	none		4 - 3
ELIJAH JOHNSON	none		4 - 4
THOMAS JOHNSON	none		3 - 3
ISAAC KILLAM	none		4 - 1
THOMAS KING	Conclusion 1500a. Sold out of above tract 73a. Longs Lott 100a. Closure 66a. Ledburn 44a.	1634a.	1 - 0
COULBOURN LONG	Longs Chance	131½a.	2 - 2
BENJAMIN LANKFORD	Boston 181a. Discovery Enlarged 63a. Snow Water 18½a. Neighbors Content 14 3/4a.	187½a.	3 - 1
WILLIAM LISTER	Listers Venture 40a. Catlins Venture 100a. Wm.s Venture	240a.	1 - 1
WILLAIM LONG	Wilsons Lott 66a. Curtis Lot 75a. Howath 100a.	241a.	3 - 3
KELLAM LANKFORD	CHance 36a. Adams Purchase 100a. Pound Pasture 17a. Bostons Purchase 355a.	508a.	4 - 1
ISAAC LANKFORD	none		3 - 2
JEFFREYLONG	Longs Delight	60a.	1 - 0
EZEKIEL LANKFORD	Vulcans Vineyard	86a.	3 - 2
DAVID LINDSEY	Boston 8a. Mumford 92a.	100a.	2 - 0
PEWSY LANKFORD	Lankfords content 81½a. Dam Quarter 36a. Plunder 13a.	130a.	2 - 3
THOMAS LISTER	none		1 - 0
JAMES LAYFIELD	none		1 - 2
ESTHER LEACH	none		1 - 5
JOSEPH LANKFORD(of John)	none		2 - 2
DAVID LANKFORDS(heirs)	Longs Chance	277½a.	0 - 0
JOSEPH LANDEN	none		4 - 4
HENRY LANDEN	none		2 - 6
RAHCEL LORD	none		1 - 3
JOHN LANDON	none		3 - 3
WILLIAM LANKFORD	none		4 - 2
JOSHUA LANKFORD	none		1 - 2
WM.LANKFORD of Wm.	none		1 - 2
GEORGE MARSHALL	none		7 - 2
HENRY MILES	Hazard 32a. Hopewell 37½a. Miles Conclusion 409a. Neglect 7a.	484½a.	5 - 4
STOUGHTON MADDOX	End of Strife 360a. Marsh Ground 50a.	410a.	6 - 4
ELZEY MADDOX	End of Strife	150a.	3 - 4
JOHN MADDOX	Inclosure	590a.	1 - 1
THOMAS MILES	Beauchamps conclusion	200a.	1 - 3
LEVIN MILES	Huntsmans Folly	288a.	3 - 1
WILLIAM MOORE	Mitchells Lott	75a.	5 - 4
JOHN MILBOURN	Milbourns Purchase	127½a.	2 - 1
STACEY MILES	Boyces Branch	80a.	2 - 2

By Thomas Handy, assessor of the GREAT ANNAMESSEX 100

OWNERS NAME	LAND	TOTAL ACRES	White-inhab. MALE-FEMALE
WILLIAM MILES	Huntsmans Folly	135a.	2 - 1
DAVID McDONALD Jr.	New Rumney	244a.	6 - 3
STEPHEN MARSHALL	Marshalls inheritance 300a. Mitchells Lott 75a. Turkey trap 44½a. Priviledge 50a. Dixons Lott 50a.	519½a.	5 - 3
THOMAS MOOR	none		4 - 2
LAZARUS MADDUX	Enlargement	9a.	1 - 4
DANEIL MADDUX	Security	140a.	3 - 2
MERRILL MADDUX	Cows Quarter & Ruscommon & Daniels Den	150a.	2 - 5
SARAH MADDUX	none		3 - 5
JAMES McCLAIN	none		1 - 0
JOHN MOOR	none		3 - 2
RISDON MARSHALL	none		3 - 2
ISAAC MILLICAN	none		3 - 1
JOHN MILLICAN	none		2 - 5
WILLIAM MILBURN	none		4 - 3
DARBY MOOR	none		2 - 1
THOMAS MITCHELL	none		1 - 2
PURNELL OUTTEN	Condoque 30a. Outtens Addition 25a. Ware Point enlarged 34a. Discovery 50a.	139a.	3 - 5
ISAAC OUTTEN	Discovery 175¼a. Webly 130a. Outtens Addition 125a. Ware point enlarged 125a. Cheesemans Chance 60a. Security 100a.	815a.	5 - 2
HENRY POTTER	Mitchells Choice 41½a. Owens Lott 100a. Mitchells Choice 188a. Cow Quarter 20a. Daniels Den 40a.	389½a.	2 - 3
THOMAS W. POTTER	Sunken ground	100a.	3 - 4
RANDAL PRYORS Heirs (by Wm.Cottingham) Mates Enjoyment 100a. Conclusion		147a.	0 - 0
JOHN PURKINS	Longs Chance	320a.	0 - 0
ARTHUR PARKS	none		6 - 2
THOMAS ROBERTSON	Neighbors Conclusion 438½a. Jones Island 100a. Conclusion of Thing 73a.	512½a.	4 - 5
JOHN REDDEN	none		3 - 2
NATHANIEL ROACH	none		3 - 3
DANIEL ROACH	none		1 - 1
BENJAMIN SCHOOLFIELD	Eilliams Green	229½a.	2 - 1
THOMAS S. SUDLER	New Invention 212a. Envy 96½a. Barnabys Lott 11¼a. Salisbury 197¼a. Trouble 50a. Littleworth 6a. Wilsons Lott 30a. Recovery 48a. Come by Chance 100a. Cow Quarter 42¼a.	793a.	1 - 0
MARY SMITH(wid/o Wm.)	Kearseys Luck 60a. Kersleys in Ernest 27½a. pt. of Condoque 44½a.	132a.	2 - 3

By Thomas Handy, assessor of the GREAT ANNAMESSEX 100

OWNERS NAME	LAND	TOTAL ACRES	White Inhab. MALE-FEMALE
ELIAS SUMMERS	none		4 - 2
SARAH SUMMERS	none		0 - 7
ISAIAH TILGHMAN	Addition 10½a. Candia Island 275½a.	286a.	0 - 0
JOSEPH TILGHMAN	Josephs Folly	66a.	0 - 0
SAMUEL TREHEARN	Dixons Lott 55a. Trehearns Lott 55a.	110a.	1 - 3
THOMAS TULL	Chance 120½a. Boston 23a. Goshen 46½a. The Desert alias Tulls purchase 154a. Winters Refuge 200a. Meadow 250a.	602a.	4 - 3
JOSHUA TULL	Hopewell 34a. Addition 70a. Beach & Pine 50a.	154a.	1 - 1
SOLOMON TULL	Wilsons Lott 24a. Waterton	26½a.	5 - 4
NEHEMIAH TURPIN	Boston 220a. Eden 95a. Conveniency 25a.	340a.	2 - 2
JOSHUA TURPIN	First Choice 39¼a. Loss & Gain 52a. Horse Hammock 152a.	243¼a.	1 - 0
WILLIAM TILGHMAN	Matthews Ridge 60a. Sapling Ridge 82a.	122a.	3 - 4
JOHN TURPIN	H. Hammock 160a. Boyces Branch 80a. Hartfords Broad Oak 26a. Catlins Venture 14a. Tottonias 149a.	369a.	3 - 4
WHITTY TURPIN	Londons Adventure & Jericho 133¼a. Good Luck 22a. Turpins Choice 367½a. Barnabys Lott 10a. Poyk 60a.	592¾a.	1 - 3
DENWOOD TURPIN	Poyk 10a. Normandy 25a. Fountains Lott 115a. Hawtree 100a. Fathers Care 90a. Hopewell 3a. Neighbors Agreement 45a.	388a.	4 - 3
SAMUEL TULL Jr.	end of Strife 90a.	90a.	3 - 3
THOMAS TULL(ofJoshua)	none		3 - 2
JOHN TREHORN	none		2 - 4
RICHARD TULL	none		1 - 2
OBED TREHORN	none		1 - 2
JAMES C. VESSELS	none		3 - 1
PLANNER WILLIAMS	Winter Harbour 100a. Cheap Price & Planners Blossom	1332a.	1 - 3
JOHN WILSON(of Samuel)	Cow Quarter 287a. Mt. Ephraim 375a. Mothers Care 705a.	1367a.	2 - 3
LEVIN WILSON	Ephraim Wilsons Land	463a.	1 - 3
JOHN WATERS	Salem 490a. New Rumney 43a. Cagers Island 700a. Teagues Addition 78a.	1311a.	0 - 0
SPENCER WATERS heirs	P. D. in the L.Choice	26 a.	0 - 0
RICHARD WATERS	Flatland 840a. Friends Kindness 116a. Waters River 525a. Conveneincy 80a. Londons Gift 50a Security 52a. Envy 70a. Miles Choice 70a.	1803a.	4 - 4

By Thomas Handy, assessor of the GREAT ANNAMESSEX 100

OWNERS NAME	LAND	TOTAL ACRES	White Inhab. MALE-FEMALE
ROSE WATERS	Waters Addition 136a. Waters River 353½a.	488½a.	0 - 2
WILLAIM WATERS Jr.	Beach and Pine 50a. Watterton 97¼a. Wilsons Lott 20a.	167¼a.	4 - 5
LEVIN WATSON	Hoggs Ridge	100a.	4 - 3
WILLIAM WILSON(of George)	Security 100a. Wilsons Purchase 21a.	121a.	3 - 4
THOMAS WILLIAMS	Williams Green 315a. Bostontown 285a.	600a.	2 - 4
JAMES WILLIS	Envy 7a. Barnabys Lott 30½a. Good Luck 53a.	90½a.	1 - 2
RHODA WILSON	Security	200a.	2 - 3
MARY WILLIAMS	Hartford Broad Oak	124½a.	0 - 5
JOHN WILLIAMS	Williams Lott 200a. Caipes Mouth 12a. First Choice 20a. North Border 400a. Conclusion 20a. Marsh Ground 30a.	682a.	1 - 1
MARY WHEATLY	The Damp Swamp 26½a. Merchants Treasure 100a. Irish Grove 100a. Wheatlys Addition 45a. Green Field 125a. Priviledge 40½a. New Boston 28 3/4a. Littleworth 3a. Adams Chance 17a.	315½a.	2 - 2
THOMAS WILLIAMS(of Jno)	Handys Purchase	59a.	1 - 2
JOHN WILSON	Vale of Misery	38a.	3 - 3
LEVIN WILLIAMS	Neighbors Conclusion 180a.	180a.	1 - 1
STEPHEN WEST	none		0 - 0
THOMAS WALSTON	none		5 - 3
JOHN WILLIAMS	none		2 - 5
LITTLETON WILLIAMS	none		3 - 2
LITTLETON WATERS	Envy 408a. Partnership	533a.	0 - 0
SARAH WATERS	none		3 - 2
WILLIAM WATERS Sr.	none		5 - 7
SARAH WALSTON	Marsh Ground	42a.	3 - 3
BETTY WINDSOR	none		2 - 2

LITTLE ANNAMESSEX 100

OWNERS NAME	LAND	TOTAL ACRES	White Inhab. MALE-FEMALE
RICHARD BRADCHER	Pitchcroft	50a.	2 - 2
THOMAS BIRD	Hills Folly	102½a.	3 - 6
SOLOMON BIRD	Unduce 127½a. Parkers Peach	241½a.	2 - 7
JOSEPHUS BELL	Expense 340a. Discovery 60a. Flatt Cap 112a.	512a.	2 - 3
MICHAEL BENSTON	none		3 - 3
MARTHA COX	Upper Undue	300a.	0 - 2
GEORGE CROSWELL	Jonathans Addition 30a. Jones Island 75a.	95a.	3 - 5
HANNAH CULLIN	none		1 - 3
ISAAC COULBOURNS heirs	Pomfret	600a.	1 - 5
SARAH COULBOURN	Pomfret	200a.	0 - 4

By Thomas Handy, assessor of LITTLE ANNAMESSEX 100

OWNERS NAME	LAND	TOTAL ACRES	White Inhab. MALE-FEMALE
ROBERT COULBOURN	None		4 - 4
WILLIAM COULBOURN	None		2 - 5
JOHN COULBOURN	none		3 - 2
WILLIAM COULBOURN Jr.	Discovery 60½a. Outlett	75a.	3 - 5
JACOB CULLIN	Cullens Lott	198a.	2 - 1
DANIEL CULLIN	Makepeace 122a. Buck Ridge	162a.	3 - 6
ELIJAH COULBOURN	Accident 37a. deed 20a. deed 6a.	63a.	1 - 4
BENJAMIN COULBOURN	Pomfret	180a.	2 - 5
LAWSON CROSWELL	none		3 - 3
THOMAS CONNOR	none		1 - 2
RICHARD CHANDLER	none		3 - 2
WILLIAM DARCUS	Watkins Point 50a. Upper Undoe 50a.	100a.	1 - 2
NATHANIEL DAUGHERTY	Usk 44a. Meads Mistake	193½a.	5 - 4
JOHN DIES	none		4 - 4
RHODA DAUGHERTY	none		2 - 4
PETER DAUGHERTY	none		1 - 0
THOMAS EVANS	Pitchcroft	100a.	3 - 6
JOHN EVANS	Pitchcroft	200a.	3 - 2
LEVIN EVANS	none		3 - 4
RICHARD EVENS	Pitchcroft	200a.	2 - 5
RICHARD EVANS Jr.	none		5 - 4
NATHAN EVANS	none		2 - 1
SOLOMON EVANS	none		1 - 1
RACHEL EVANS	none		0 - 3
KIRK GUNBY	none		1 - 0
JOHN GUNBY Sr.	Middle Ridge 248a. Chance 250a. Kirks Chance 32a. Flatcap 25a. Davis's Lott 100a.	416a.	3 - 5
SARAH GUNBY	1/3rd of afsd land	138a.	0 - 1
JAMES GUNBY	Kirks Purchase 200a. Gunbys Pasture 75a. Meadow 100a. Usk 82a. Low Swamp 100a. Littleworth 40a. Gunbys Conclusion 3½a.	600½a.	2 - 1
WILLIAM HENDERSON	Pomfret	83a.	1 - 1
ROBERT HOLLAND	Hollands Chance 50a. Ferry Bridge100a.	150a.	1 - 1
LEVI HOLLAND	none		1 - 2
JOHN HORSEY	Watkins Point, Horseys Down & Horseys Lott	260a.	2 - 3
SARAH HORSEY	Watkins Point 150a. Brickle House 250a.	400a.	2 - 3
EDWARD HOLLAND	none		3 - 5
JAMES HEARN	Scotland	185a.	3 - 3
MICHAEL HOLLAND	Hollands Chance 166a. Pomfret 45a. Pomfret 27a.	248a.	3 - 4
THOMAS HANDY Sr.	Davis Good will	663a.	4 - 4
STEPHEN HOPKINS	none		2 - 2
BENJAMIN HOPKINS	none		2 - 2
ISAAC HOPKINS	none		3 - 3
MARTHA HANDY	none		0 - 0

By Thomas Handy, assessor of LITTLE ANNAMESSEX 100

OWNERS NAME	LAND	TOTAL ACRES	White MALE	Inhab. FEMALE
JOHN KILLIAM Jr.	Chance 50a. Addition 14½a. Dickersons Folly 100a.	164½a.	5	5
JOHN KNISSE	Cork	8a.	1	2
JOHN KILLIAM Sr.	none		1	2
JOHN JOHNSON Sr.	Rich Swamp 50a. Doe Park 50a. Last Choice 67a.	157a.	3	3
ISAAC JOHNSON	Cabbin Swamp & Exchange	60a.	2	5
LITTLETON JOHNSON	none		2	3
MARY JUETT	none		0	1
NATHANIEL JUETT	Hopewell 36a. Moreworth 8a. More Still 220a. Emmecks 100a. Hogland Quarter 12a. Worthless 4a.	438a.	5	3
LAZARUS LANKFORD (heirs.)	nones unknown	200a.	0	0
ELIJAH LINTON	Pitchcraft	25a.	5	2
SAMUEL LAWSON Sr.	Hills Folly	47a.	1	1
THOMAS LORD Jr.	Chestnut Ridge	75a.	2	6
JOHN LAWSON	none		2	1
THOMAS LORD	none		3	3
POTTER LORD	none		1	4
HANCE LAWSON	none		3	3
BENJAMIN LANKFORD Jr.	Watkins Point	94½a.	4	1
SAMUEL LAWSON Jr.	Cork 50a. White Oak 12a.	62a.	3	2
SAMUEL LONG	Beards Neck	100a.	1	1
SARAH LONG	Come by Chance 100a. Hogs Hammock 100a. Longs Chance	225a.	0	1
HENRY MILES	Hearts ease	250a.	5	4
JACOB MILBOURN	Undoe 108a. Jones Island	133a.	5	4
MARMADUKE MISTER	Pitchcroft	100a.	2	6
ALCE McCENNY	none		1	1
ISAAC MOORE	Bay Bush Hall	60a.	4	3
DENNIS MONTGOMERY	none		4	4
MARY MOORE	Dublin	25a.	3	1
JOHN MOORE	Maddux Hope	100a.	4	3
WILLIAM MILES	Hearts Ease?(blotted)	125a.	3	1
WILLIAM MERRILL	Scotland	117a.	1	0
RACHEL MASON	none		3	2
MARY PARREMORE	none		0	1
JOHN PARKS	Pitchcroft	130a.	3	3
CHARLES PAUL	none		2	2
JOHN PARKS Sr.	none		1	1
JOHN RIGGIN	Cabin Swamp	100a.	2	3
DUKES RIGGIN	Emmessex 50a. Littleworth	100a.	3	4
JONATHAN RIGGIN	Cork	25a.	1	2
WILLIAM RIGGIN Jr.	none		5	3
RACHEL ROACH	MakePeace 50a. Exchange 16a. Force Putt 46a. Muirsland 12a.	124a.	0	2
WILLIAM ROACH	Makepeace 100a. Exchange 34a. ForcePutt 92a. Cabin Swamp 14a. Half Quarter 35a. Meadsland 22a.	297a.	3	1

By Thomas Handy, assessor of LITTLE ANNAMESSEX 100

OWNERS NAME	LAND	TOTAL ACRES	White Inhab. MALE-FEMALE
JONATHAN ROACH	Longtown 40a. Lott 12a. Johnsons Lott 63a. Meads land 32a.	166a.	4 - 5
TRAVES STERLING	Wards Folly 16½a. Cedar Hammock 20a. unknown 40a.	76½a.	2 - 2
ROBERT RIGGIN	none		4 - 4
WILLIAM RIGGIN	none		1 - 2
STEPHEN RIGGEN	none		1 - 2
MARY STERLING	Starlings Chance 50a. Puzzle 25a. Sterlings Chance 32a. Longtown 17¼a. Sterlings fancy 9a. Stansteads Abby 50a.	129½a.	0 - 1
AARON STERLING	Haphazard 70a. Industry 5a. Sterlings Chance 20a. Comicle Joke 26a. Cabin Swamp 10a. Exchange 72½a. Good Luck 50a. Barnet 30a. Troublesome 50a. Marsh 14a. Priviledge 2½a. Oak Hammock 100a. Stansby Abbe 40a.	490a.	2 - 2
HENRY STERLING	Apes Hole 160a. Jamestown?	185a.	3 - 4
JONATHAN SUMMERS	Emmessex	60½a.	3 - 2
THOMAS SUMMERS	Emmexxex	60½a.	3 - 5
ISAAC SUMMERS	Longtown	80a.	3 - 4
DAVID SUMMERS	Emmessex	90a.	2 - 4
RICHARD SUMMERS	Emmessex	90a.	1 - 1
HENRY STERLING Jr.	none		3 - 4
LAZARUS SUMMERS	none		4 - 4
LITTLETON STERLING	none		2 - 6
JOHN STERLING	none		2 - 5
BETTY SUMMERS	none		2 - 2
GEORGE SUMMERS	none		4 - 4
JAMES SUMMERS	none		2 - 4
MOSES SUMMERS	none		5 - 4
LEVI THOMAS	Jones Island	130a.	3 - 4
JOHN TAWS	Cork	15a.	3 - 3
THOMAS TYLOR	Pitchcraft	200a.	5 - 4
WILLIAM THOMAS	none		2 - 3
JOHN WARD	none		2 - 1
SARAH WHITE	none		0 - 1
MARY WARD	none		0 - 2
STEPHEN WARD(of Mathias)	none		3 - 3
JOHN WARD Sr.	Cork 100a. Littleworth 40a. Long Acre 50a.	190a.	1 - 2
STEPHEN WARD(of John)	Little Bolton	75a.	2 - 4
CORNELUIS Ward Sr.	Cork 25a. Folly 9½a. White Oak Swamp 25a. Prices Conclusion 75a. Long Acre 20a.	134½a.	2 - 2
JAMES WARD	Cork 25a. Folly 9½a. White Oak Swamp 25a. Prices Conclusion 75a. Long Acre 20a.	154½a.	1 - 0
SOUTHY WHITTINGTON	unknown	700a.	0 - 0

By Thomas Handy, assessor of LITTLE ANNAMESSEX 100

OWNERS NAME	LAND	TOTAL ACRES	White Inhab. MALE-FEMALE
STEPHEN WARD	Prices vineyard 100a. Agreement 50a. Middle of the Neck Addition 30a. Wards Conclusion 69a. Bostons Lott 30a. Long Town 50a. Hopewell 33a. Harts Ease 192a. Mickel Meadow 75a.	568½a.	2 - 3
THOMAS WARD	Prices Vineyard 50a. Jamestown 100a. Quarter Agreement 53a. Apes Hole 8a. Mickle Meadow 75a.	257a.	6 - 5
WILLIAM WHITTINGTON	Chance 79a. Recovery 125a. Puzzle 170a.	374a.	4 - 3
MARY WARD	none		0 - 2
MARY WHITTINGTON	none		0 - 2
ISAAC WHITTINGTON	Addition 100a. Chance 70a. Recovery 125a.	295a.	4 - 2
WILLIAM WARD	Cork	50a.	2 - 5
MATHIAS WARD	Littleworth	57a.	2 - 2
SAMUEL WARD	Cork	50a.	4 - 3
ANN WARD	Last of Cork 25a. Long Acre 250a. White Oak Swamp 50a.	325a.	1 - 5
WILLIAM WILSON	Littleworth 25a. Victory 5½a.	30½a.	2 - 2
WILLIAM WHEATLY	Cabin Swamp	75a.	1 - 1
EZEKIEL WARD	Doublin 50a. unknown 25a.	75a.	3 - 1
JOHN WILLIAMS	Little Bolton & Unknown	850a.	1 - 3
ISAAC WARD	none		1 - 2

POCOMOKE 100

OWNERS NAME	LAND	TOTAL ACRES	White Inhab. MALE-FEMALE
HOPE ADDAMS	The Adventure	105a.	4 - 3
WILLIAM ADDAMS	Haphazard 8¼a. Addams Conclusion 250a.	258¼	3 - 2
SAMUEL ADDAMS	Adams Folly 301a. Elgates Irish Grove 150a. Shoemakers Meadow 20a. Haphazard 12½a. Collins Adventure 139a.	622½a.	0 - 0
EPHRAIM ADDAMS	Kings Lott 204a. Adams Garden 50a. Adams Green 50a.	304a.	1 - 0
SARAH ADAMS	Adams Garden, Haphazard & Kings Lott	108¼a.	2 - 3
ISAAC ADDAMS	Carsleys Industry 147a. Discovery & Meadow 62½a.	209½a.	3 - 3
WILLIAM ADDAMS Sr.	Mentwell 140a. Haphazard 8¼a.	148¼a.	1 - 2
SARAH ADDAMS	Chance 60a. Haphazard 5a.	65a.	1 - 3
GERTRUDE ADAMS	Houstons Choice 160a. Discovery 22a. Adventure 70a. Snow Hill 178a. Adams Purchase 50a.	480a.	1 - 3
MARY ADDAMS	Adams Conclusion	140a.	0 - 2
WILLIAM ADDAMS Jr.	Mentwell	100a.	4 - 1
GEORGE ADDAMS	Adventure	75a.	4 - 4
SABRAH ADDAMS	Long Ridge & Adventure	125a.	0 - 2
JOSEPH BEEL	Matthews Adventure	25a.	1 - 4
FOUNTAIN BEAUCHAMP	The Adventure	5a.	3 - 2

By Thomas Handy, assessor of POCOMOKE 100

OWNERS NAME	LAND	TOTAL ACRES	White Inhab. MALE-FEMALE
RHODA BEAUCHAMP	The Adventure	60a.	2 - 3
LEVI BEAUCHAMP	none		3 - 2
WILLIAM BROUGHTON Jr.	none		2 - 1
DANIEL BOSTON	Crookes Island	1a.	2 - 2
STEPHEN COULBOURN	Adams Garden 75a. Kings Lott 125a.	200a.	3 - 3
ABIGAIL COLLINS	Collins Addition 344a. Smyth Collin's 100a.	444a.	2 - 1
WILLIAM COX	Waterford 450a. Coxes Bill 35a. Angelsia 100a.	585a.	3 - 3
SAMUEL COLLINS	none		1 - 0
WILLIAM CAMEL	none		3 - 2
MARTHA COTTHAM	none		0 - 2
JAMES DYCKES	Buck Ridge 150a. Hignols Choice 150a.	300a.	2 - 3
CATHERINE DICKERSON	Late Discovery 200a. Cambells Lott 11a.	211a.	0 - 3
JESSE DYKES	none		3 - 4
EPHRAIM EVENS	Oyster Whell point 9a. Owing Lindors	109a.	1 - 3
SPENCER EVENS	none		3 - 3
THOMAS EVENS	none		1 - 0
NEOMI GILES	none		0 - 0
JESSE HALL	Addition to Tully Brisk 42a. Tully Brisk 13a.	55a.	7 - 2
WILLIAM HALL	Pimore 200a. Liverty 112a.	212a.	3 - 4
ROBERT J. HENRY	Mary's Lott 400a. Manloves Lott 158a. Henrys Addition 50a. Limbrick 133½a. Glasgow 72a. Land in Rehobeth town 10a. Conviency 134½a. Whitteys Rectified 245a. Long Meadow 626a. Goose Marsh 50a. Cow Marsh 50a. Dickersons Hope 125½a.	2054¼a.	1 - 3
JACOB HERN	none		6 - 5
WILLIAM HAYLEY	none		5 - 3
WILLIAM HUTCHING	none		3 - 3
JOHN JURDIENS Heirs	unknown	49½a.	0 - 0
WILLIAM KERSEY	Venture	90a.	2 - 2
PETER KERSEY	Discovery, Irish Grove & Carsleys Industry	129a.	4 - 3
DUNKIN LEVENSTON	The Adventure	94a.	4 - 3
SOLOMON McCREADY	Matthews Adventure 35a. McCreadys First Choice 17a. Wrangle 18a.	70a.	2 - 2
ELIJAH MATTHEWS	Sons Choice	100a.	1 - 0
ISAAC McCREDDY	First Choice	100a.	3 - 2
ROBERT MARSHALL	Tasseo	150a.	2 - 5
TABITHA MERCHANT	Handys Hall	60a.	2 - 4
JONATHAN MILBOURN	Prices Grove 150a. Lindsays Green 50a.	200a.	5 - 2

By Thomas Handy, ass essor of POCOMOKE 100

OWNERS NAME	LAND	TOTAL ACRES	White Inhab. MALE-FEMALE
ISAAC MARSHALL	Dixons Lott 50a. Bostons Purchase 200a. Bostons Green 25a. Bostons Chance 240½a. Shoemakers Meadow 39a. Sawards Purchase 19 3/4a.	573¾a.	3 - 6
LODOWICK MILBOURN	Crooked Island 4a. Dales Adventure 100a. Handys Hall 40a. Prices Grove 77a.	221a.	2 - 4
DAVID MATTHEWS Sr.	Cow Quarter 100a. Golden Lion 150a. Golden Lion 235a.	485a.	4 - 3
SAMUEL MATTHEWS Jr.	Edwin 40a. Matthews Delight 35a. Ellis Lott 50a.	125a.	5 - 9
DAVID MATTHEWS Jr.	Edwin 100a. Meadow 15a. Haphazard 12a.	127a.	4 - 4
SAMUEL MATTHEWS Sr.	Edwin 100a. Meadow 25a.	125a.	1 - 1
ANDREW McCREADY	Matthews Adventure	25a.	2 - 3
WILLIAM MILLS	none		2 - 1
BAILEY MATTHEWS	none		6 - 3
JACOB MATTHEWS	none		2 - 4
MATTHEW McNIDERS	(Henry James Harper exec. Estate)	0a.	0 - 0
BENJAMIN MATTHEWS	Worthless 100a. Haphazard	112a.	2 - 2
BOAZ MATTHEWS	none		3 - 3
SUSAY MILBOURN	Prices Grove 150a. Venter 80a.	230a.	2 - 3
JOHN MARCHANT	none		4 - 2
CALEB MILBOURN	none		2 - 2
ELEANOR NAIRNE	Nairns Addition 57a. Pemore 100a. Jerry 45a.	202a.	2 - 3
OBED RIGGIN	Golden Lion 100a. Riggins Meadow 50a.	150a.	2 - 4
TEAGUE RIGGIN	Meadow Ground 100a. Riggins amendment 210a.	310a.	4 - 6
JEMMINAH RIGGIN	Prices Conclusion 25a. Riggins Amendemnt 75a.	100a.	0 - 2
LEVI RIGGIN	Riggins Mind 100a. Dickersons Hope 40a. Costons Bay side 59½a.	199½a.	4 - 2
NATHANIEL RIGGIN	Green Park	200a.	3 - 3
STEPHEN RIGGIN	none		4 - 4
SARAH TAYLOR	Dublin	70a.	0 - 1
JOHN TULL	none		3 - 2
ISAAC B. SCHOOLFIELD	Rehobeth 97a. Oak Hall 90a. Hogg yard 23a.	220a.	2 - 1
GEORGE SCHOOLFIELD	Rehobeth	100a.	2 - 4
JOHN SCHOOLFIELD	Rehobeth	100a.	1 - 1
HENRY SCHOOLFIELD	Chance 51a. Addition to Chance 30a. Hogg yard 7 and 3 ½a.	91½a.	2 - 2
STEPHEN SCHOOLFIELD	none		2 - 4
LEAH SCHOOLFIELD	none		1 - 2
JOHN SMALL	none		4 - 2
WILLIAM WADDEY	Entrance	500a.	2 - 3
JESSE WARD	Owens Glendore	50a.	3 - 2

By Thomas Handy assessor of POCOMOKE 100

OWNERS NAME	LAND	TOTAL ACRES	White Inhab. MALE-FEMALE
JOSEPH WILSON	none		3 - 3
THOMAS WILSON	Addition to Tully Brisk 14a. Support 13a.	27a.	3 - 2
WILLIAM WHITE Sr.	Addition to Tully Brisk 50a. Discovery 11a. Priviledge 15a. Tully Brisk 45¼a.	111¼a.	2 - 3
WILLIAM WOOD	Woods Contention 151a. Bostons Adventure 41a. Dubling 92a.	284a.	3 - 4
WILLIAM WARD	Handys Meadow and Owen Glendore	158a.	3 - 4
MARTHA WILLIAMS	Willings Green	488a.	1 - 4
ZADOCK WHEALLER	Calf Pasture	212a.	0 - 0
ANN WHITE	Isaacs Fortune 249a. Long Acre 12a.	260a.	1 - 3
ARCHIBLAD WHITE (16 yrs.)	none		0 - 0
SARAH WETMON	cone		0 - 2

DIVIDING CREEK 100

OWNERS NAME	LAND	TOTAL ACRES	White Inhab. MALE-FEMALE
PHILLIP C. ADAMS	Adams Purchase 200a. Beckles 10a. Norfolk 200a.	410a.	4 - 3
PHILLIP ADAMS	New Wood Hall 94¼a. Wood Hall 8a. Hog quarter 13a. Haphazard 5a.	120¼a.	6 - 5
PHILLIP ADAMS(of Hope)	Ledburn 117a. Beauchamps Venture 44a. Haphazard 5a.	166a.	3 - 3
SAMUEL ADAMS	Beckles 93a. Chance 50a. Norfolk 50a. Adams Purchase 327½a.	520½a.	4 - 4
ESAU BOSTON	none		2 - 0
THOMAS BEAUCHAMP	Beauchamps Venture	173½a.	2 - 4
JOHN BROUGHTON Jr.	Williams Hope 100a. Blakes Hope 53 1/3a.	153⅓a.	4 - 2
ELIJAH BROUGHTON	none		2 - 1
BENSTON BLADES	Newtown	110a.	2 - 0
JOSHUA BEAUCHAMP	Ledburn 175a. Beauchamps venture 25a. Adams Conclusion 59a.	259a.	4 - 5
LEVIN BEAUCHAMP	Beauchamps enture	241 1/3a.	3 - 3
JOHN BEAUCHAMP	Ledbourn 175a. Hog Yard 26a. Addition to conclusion 57a.	252a.	1 - 5
THOMAS BRUFF	Caldicott	250a.	
JOHN BROUGHTON Sr.	Broughtons Purchase 114a. Addition 36a. Timbertract 21a. Newtown 4½a. Tilghmans Care 76a. Williams Hope 21a.	274a.	3 - 5
THOMAS BENSTON	Green Meadow 30a. Exchange 31a. Dreadens Destiny 180a.	230a.	3 - 4
Rev. HAMILTON BELL	Chance 10a. Cypress Swamp 20a. Little Derry 160a.	190a.	0 - 0

By Thomas Handy assessor of DIVIDING CREEK 100.

OWNERS NAME	LAND	TOTAL ACRES	White Inhab. MALE-FEMALE
EDWARD BEAUCHAMP	none		4 - 5
THOMAS W. BENSTON	none		1 - 2
ELIJAH BEAUCHAMP	Hogyard 25a. Ledburn 70a. Three Brothers 205a.)	330a.	1 - 6
KILLIAM BROUGHTON	none		3 - 2
JOHN BEAUCHAMP	none		2 - 1
CHARLES BROUGHTON	none		1 - 1
LAZARUS BOSTON	none		1 - 2
SARAH COSTON	Baltimore 32a. Addition to Beech Ridge 13a. Costons Trouble, Flatlands, Costons Vineyard Bear Point	69¼a.	2 - 5
BENJAMIN COTTMAN	Beech Ridge 38¼a. Costons Vineyard 52a. Costons Venture 19a.	114¼a.	2 - 2
JONATHAN CLUFF	Neglect 149 1/3a. Timber grove 37a.	341½a.	6 - 2
MATHIAS COSTON	Costons Trouble 397a. Addn. to Beech Ridge 135a.	532a.	3 - 1
JOSEPH COTTMAN	Addn. to Beech Ridge, Costons Venture, Winter Range, Baltimore Glade Swamp	553a.	4 - 1
MICHAEL CLUFF	Blakes Hope 233a. Timber Grove 37½a. Newtown 21a. Hakcelay	341½a.	3 - 2
JAMES DREDDEN	Hackley 80a. Timber Grove 30a.	110a.	2 - 1
RACHEL DREDDEN	none		0 - 3
ZADOCK DORMAN	Dormans Discovery	89a.	1 - 0
KATHERINE DORMAN	Dormans Discovery	43a.	0 - 2
THOMAS DREDDEN	Powells Chance	50a.	2 - 4
BEAUCHAMP DAVIS	Ledbourn 45a. Mitchells Lott 37½a. Beauchamp Venture 21a. Addn. to Adventure 76a.	249¼a.	5 - 3
SUSANNAH DENNIS	Rehobeth 26a. Caldicuit 475a. Conclusion 50a. Exchange 30a.	631a.	0 - --
LITTLETON DREDDEN	Drydens Destiny 100a. Hog range 30a. Powells Chance 115½a.	245½a.	5 - 3
LEVIN DORMAN	Chance 80a. Dormans Purchase	286a.	5 - 4
ALEXANDER DEAN	unknown	250a.	0 - 0
BETTY DREDDEN	none		1 - 2
ELIAS DEER	none		3 - 4
SARAH DENSTON	none		1 - 2
ELIAKIM DUBLING	none		1 - 1
ARTHUR DORWICK	noen		2 - 1
WILSON DORMAN	none		2 - 2
GEORGE FURNIS	none		2 - 5
JOHN FLEMING	Unity enlarged	340a.	2 - 4
WILLIAM FLEMING	Middleton 136a. Harris's Adventure 30a. Harris's venture 50a. Flemings inclusion 275a. Flemings Loss	480a.	3 - 3
THOMAS FISHER	none		2 - 3
WILLIAM FOURDS	none		3 - 3
SPENCER HARRIS	Harris's venture 150a. Harris's Chance 150a. Prevention 112a.	312a.	3 - 5
JAMES HOLLAND	none		2 - 4

By Thomas Handy, assessor of DIVIDING CREEK 100

OWNERS NAME	LAND	TOTAL ACRES	White Inhab. MALE-FEMALE
RHODA HALL	Baltimore 30a. Bare Point 120a.	150a.	2 - 5
JOHN HARRIS	Chance 316a. Pasturage 30a. Hog Quarter 10a. Nights Sucess 13a. Turkey Trap 5a. several surveys without patent 26a. Harris Adventure 312a.	692a.	5 - 2
THOMAS HAYWARD	Haywards Lot 740a. Blakes Hope 100a. Ireland 250a.	1094a.	5 - 5
WILLIAM HAMMOND	none		2 - 5
LITTLETON HARRIS	none		3 - 4
SARAH HARRIS	Flemings Loss 30a. Flemings Conclusion 17a. Middleton	137a.	2 - 2
JOHN HANDY	Middlesex	100a.	2 - 6
JAMES HALL	Chance & Beauchamps Venture	20a.	4 - 2
STEPEN HATH	none		1 - 5
ROBERT J. KING	Timber tract 500½a. Plague without Profit, Tilghmans Care 350½a. Tilghmans Security Broughtons Purchase	900¼a.	3 - 4
BETTY KNIGHT	none		0 - 2
DAVID LONG	Cow Quarter 30a. Wood Hall 105a. Adventure 100a. New Wood Hall	305a.	3 - 4
WILLIAM MILES(of Samuel)	Waterford 65a. Miles Lott 80a.	150a.	0 - 0
THOMAS N. MADDUX	Newtown 60a. Tilghmans Care	83a.	2 - 1
STEPHEN MILLS	Suffolk	275a.	5 - 7
JANE MITCHELL	Middlesex 350a. Williams Hope 69a	269a.	1 - 4
JACOB MERRILL	none		5 - 1
JOHN MITCHELL	Suffolk 20½a. Neighbors Neglect 53a. Good Success (Addition to) 177a.	366a.	3 - 4
STEPHEN MITCHELL	Littleworth 42½a. Mitchells purchase 157a.	199½a.	3 - 1
MATHIAS MILES	Hap at a Venture 80a. Discovery 20a. Neglect 110a. Ridge 50a.	270a.	0 - 0
WILLIAM MATTHEWS	Knights Sucess	95a.	2 - 2
LEVIN MADDUX	Costins Vineyard 32¼a. Baltimore 26a. Beech Ridge 20¼a.	78 ½a.	3 - 4
MARY MILES	Outlett 30a. Hackley 50a. Discovery 55½a. Knights Sucess 25½a. Littleworth 7a. Grays Purchase 492 resurvey 21¼a.	770½a.	2 - 1
BETTY MATTHEWS	none		1 - 2
ELIJAH MOORE	none		3 - 3
JAMES McCAN	none		2 - 1
WILLIAM MATTHEWS	none		4 - 0
JOHN PEACOCK	none		1 - 2
JOHN PURKINS	Little Profit 103a. Hog Quarter 18½a. Newtown 240a.	315½a.	2 - 4
Jesse Powell	Powells Adventure 30a. Green Field 180a.	210a.	2 - 4

By Thomas Handy, assessor of DIVIDING CREEK 100

OWNERS NAME	LAND	TOTAL ACRES	White Inhab. MALE-FEMALE
JOHN PADEN	CHANCE 20a. Timber Grove 30a. Hackilah 661a. Quarter 20a.	731a.	5 - 2
BRITIAN POWELL	Wood Hall 198a. Hog Quarter 71a.	269a.	6 - 6
JOHN PORTER	Kings Glad 54a. Tick Ridge 23a. Purchase 319a.	391a.	2 - 2
LEVI POWELL	Greenfield Lott 40a. Hickory Ridge 19a.	59a.	1 - 0
JOHN PHILLIPS	Dudly 50a. Priviledge 50a. Rowley Hill 100a. Grays Purchase 100a. Security 30a. Phillips Conclusion 389½a.	739a.	3 - 1
JOHN POLLITT	Smyths Folly 75a. Deer Quarter 160a. Veckles 40a. Costons Second Adventure 217¼a.	296¼a.	2 - 2
RACHEL POWELL	Cow Quarter 5a. Gum Neck 25a. Greenfield 6a.	36a.	0 - 2
LEVIN POWELL	Cow Quarter 11a. Gum Neck 47a. Greenfield 13a.	71a.	1 - 0
JOHN PEWSEY	Winsor Castle 100a. Addition 251a.	351a.	4 - 5
JOHN PILCHER	none		2 - 1
TEAGUE RIGGEN	Middle Plantation 160a. Last Choice 18a. Flemings Conclusion 9a.	187a.	2 - 5
NEIL RICHEY	Baltimore 90a. Ware Point	177a.	1 - 3
LEVIN REVEL	none		1 - 2
JOHN RIGGIN	Friends Choice 18a. Pastuarage 8a. Venture 238a. Bares point 125a.	389a.	3 - 4
HUGH REESE	none		3 - 3
SAMUEL SLOAN	Williams Hope 137a. Chance 15a. Good Sucess 150a.	302a.	1 - 2
SAMUEL SMYTH	Smyths Lot 90a. Bad Luck 10a. Huntsmans Folly 35a. Miles Lott 24a.	179a.	5 - 3
NATHANIEL SMULLEN	Goshen 100a. Unity Enlarged	149a.	4 - 6
EDWARD SMYTH	Patricks Folly	118a.	2 - 3
LEAH SMULLEN	Goshen 100a. Unity Enlarged	149a.	0 - 6
WILLIAM SUMMERS	none		2 - 1
MARY STEVENS	Blakes Hope	66a.	0 - 2
WILLIAM STEVENS	Blakes Hope	134a.	1 - 1
SAMUEL MILES	Bad Luck 122a. Miles Purchase 442a. Glade Swamp 190a. Miles Lott 81a.	665a.	1 - 2
SAMUEL TULL	Tulls Addition	212a.	2 - 3
ISAIAH TILGHMAN	Tilmans Fortune 90a. Tilmans Enlargement 1150a. Waterford 50a. Middle Pasture	1182a.	0 - 0
AARON TILGHMAN	none		2 - 2

By Thomas Handy, assessor of DIVIDING CREEK 100

OWNERS NAME	LAND	TOTAL ACRES	White Inhab MALE-FEMALE
JOHN TULL(of Richard)	none		2 - 2
JONATHAN TULL Jr.	Colemans Adventure 133a. Tulls Adventure 13a.	146a.	2 - 1
WILLIAM TAYLOR	Plague without Profit 43a. Gideons Luck 41½a.	84½a.	4 - 3
HANNAH TILGHMAN	Blakes Hope 33 1/3a.	33 1/3a.	1 - 2
WILLIAM TAYLOR	none		2 - 2
SAMUEL WILSON	Acquintica 338a. Friendship 100a Exchange & Middle 96a. His Own before 10a. Cow Pasture 112a. Calf Pasture 27a.	733a.	0 - 0
LEAH WARD	none		0 - 1
GEORGE WATERS	Suffolk 446½a. Hakala resurv. 75a. Waters Addn. enlargement 165 Watters Addn. 11a.	697a.	4 - 2
EDWARD WATERS	Hogyard 50a. Whartons Folly & Timber tract	988a.	1 - 2
STEPHEN WARD	Harmsworth 317a. Hammock	367a.	4 - 5
JOSIAH WARWICK	none		1 - 1
SOLOMON WARD	unknown	135a.	4 - 4
ELIZABETH WARD	Paxon Hill, Little Swamp & Hog Quarter	85a.	2 - 2
JOSEPH WARD	unknown		2 - 4
JESSE WARD	Come by Chance 80a. Littleworth 25a.	105a.	2 - 2
WILLIAM S. WHITE	Rehobeth 550a. Caldicott	650a.	1 - 0
WILLIAM WARWICK Sr.	Harpers Discovery 100a. Warwicks Discovery 121a. Little Swamp & Whittingtons neglect 7a. Purchase 50a.	278a.	6 - 4
WILLIAM WARWICK Jr.	Warwicks Discovery 50a.	50a.	1 - 0
SARAH WARD	none		0 - 4
MATTHEWS WARD	none		5 - 2

END OF SOMERSET COUNTY

1783 Tax List of Worcester County

By William Richardson assessor of PITTS CREEK 100

OWNERS NAME	LAND	TOTAL ACRES	White Inhab MALE-FEMALE
ANN ADDAMS	Cowley 134a. Desire 100a.	234a.	0 - 3
WILLIAM AYDELOTTE	Refuge	297½a.	0 - 0
NABOTH BOSTON	Cowley	100a.	2 - 3
SAMUEL BLADES	Kickotan Choice	100a.	4 - 6
JACOB BOSTON	Bostons Hardship	161a.	3 - 4
ISAAC BRITTINGHAM	(young man, John Houston Security)		1 - 0
ELIJAH Brittingham	(young man, " " ")		1 - 0
ZEPHANIAH BENSTON	Partnership 14a. Last of All	126a.	2 - 7
PURNELL BRITTINGHAM	Addition 57½a. Merrills Hall 30a.	87½a.	5 - 4
JEHU BLADES	Repentance 65a. True Bridge 50a.	65a.	5 - 2
SAMUEL BLADES	Security	106½a.	5 - 5
ELIJAH BOSTON	none		3 - 2
JOHN BENSTON	(young man-Jon.t Patterson Secruity)		1 - 0
JOHN BURSHALL	none		3 - 1
JOHN BUCHANNON	(Mrs. Susannah Dennis Security)		1 - 0
ELIZABETH BLADES	none		0 - 2
ESAU BOSTON	none		3 - 1
LEVENIA BLADES	Adventure	50a.	1 - 1
STEPHEN BEAUCHAMP	none		4 - 4
SARAH BURNETT	Wooten Underedge 50a. James Security 57a.	107a.	1 - 2
ELIJAH BURNETT	Burnetts Venture 60a. Bradshers Purchase 11a.	71a.	1 - 4
WILLIAM CAREY	Truebridge	50a.	3 - 4
LEVI CAREY	none		7 - 3
JOHN C. CROPPER	unknown	200a.	0 - 0
CILAS CHAPMAN	Poor Hall	50a.	2 - 3
HANNAH CONNER	none		0 - 2
NOBLE DRYDEN	True Bridge	50a.	3 - 5
SUSANNAH DENNIS	Security alias Assumption 250a. Standleys 350a.	600a.	2 - 3
HANDY TULL	Myrtle Has?	100a.	3 - 3
LITTLETON TAYLOR	(young man Jonas Layfield Security)		1 - 0
JAMES TULL	Peterborough 40a.	40a.	3 - 2
	------------ James Security 33¼a. Bratchers Purchase 35a.	157a.	
JAMES VIRDIN	Saltum_? Townsends Mistake 1st. Quarter 265a.	370a.	2 - 2
SOLOMON WEBB	True Bridge 216a. Winter Quarter 90a. Discovery 39a.	345a.	1 - 2
ZADOCK WHEELER	Cherryston	120a.	6 - 4
WILLIAM WARRANTON	none		1 - 2
MAJOR WATSON	none		3 - 1
JONATHAN WEST WATSON Jr.	Poor Hall 125a.	125a.	3 - 6
SOLOMON WEBB	Repentance	150a.	1 - 2
DANIEL YOUNG	Adventure 100a. Costons Choice 50a. Orphan Branch	250a.	3 - 2
JOHN YOUNG	Small tract	250a.	3 - 7
EZEKIEL YOUNG	Mt. Pleasant	100a.	2 - 5
DANIEL YOUNG	(young man-Daniel Young Security)		1 - 0
EPHRAIM YOUNG	none		1 - 3

By William Richardson, assessor of PITTS CREEK 100

OWNERS NAME	LAND	TOTAL ACRES	White Inhab. MALE-FEMALE
MILBY YOUNG	unknown	2½a.	1 - 1
PEGG YOUNG	none		1 - 2
HENRY DENNIS Esq.	Pittsborough	1655½a.	1 - 0
NEHEMIAH DICKERSON	Hog Quarter	100a.	7 - 3
BENJAMIN DAVIS	Davis Refuge	49a.	4 - 3
MAJOR DAVIS(Young man-Benjamin Davis Security)			1 - 0
JAMES DAVIS	Meltons Discovery, Davis Choice Savis Liberty 50a.	242a.	0 - 0
ESTHER DAVIS	none		2 - 2
JOSHUA DICKERSON	Poor Hall 75a. Priviledge 25a.	100a.	1 - 2
WILLIAM ELLIS	Poor Hall	100a.	3 - 4
ABNER ELLIS	none		3 - 5
JESSEE ELLIS	Watsons Misfortune 20a. Honest Purchase 50a.	70a.	3 - 3
LEVI ELLIS	Chance 36a. Honest Purchase	46a.	2 - 2
SARAH GILLETT	Gilletts Chance	200a.	0 - 2
WILLIAM GILLETT	Kingsland	140a.	1 - 1
AYRES GILLETT	Level Ridge Enlarged	375a.	1 - 0
BENJAMIN HENDERSON	Timber grove 110a. Resurvey ditto 90a. Haphazard 70a.	270a.	4 - 4
EPHRAIM HENDERSON	Haphazzard 99a. Hendersons Folly 60a.	159a.	0 - 0
LEVI HOUSTON	Chestnut Ridge	33a.	3 - 3
SMART HENDERSON	none		1 - 2
JOHN HOUSTON	Chestnut Ridge	70a.	3 - 5
JOSEPH HOUSTON	Scotts Lott 100a. Langston 150a. Brittinghams Chance 91a.	241a.	4 - 5
FRANCIS HOUSTON	Last of All	114a.	3 - 5
BROADWATER HILL	none		1 - 2
BABEL HILL	Jacobs Lott	100a.	2 - 2
AARON HUDSON Jr.	True Bridge	93a.	2 - 7
EBENEZER HANDCOCK	none		4 - 1
WILLIAM HENDERSON	none		1 - 2
JENKINS HENDERSON	none		3 - 2
ROBERT JENKINS HENRY	Roberts Addition to Fair Meadow 300a. Fair Meadow Rectified 535a.	835a.	0 - 0
JAMES HENDERSON	Double Purchase	192a.	1 - 2
THOMAS HENDERSON	none		4 - 2
WILLIAM HENDERSON	Double Purchase 117½a. Conviency 125a.	242½a.	2 - 3
JARVIS HOUSTON (young man. Wm. Henderson Security)			1 - 0
JOSEPH HENDERSON	Double Purchase	160a.	1 - 3
LEVI HENDERSON	none		1 - 0
SARAH HENDERSON	none		0 - 3
WM HOLLAND HENDERSON(young man, Joseph Henderson Sec.)			1 - 0
JOHN HENDERSON	none		2 - 2
JACOB HENDERSON	Landing Purchase 120a. Barron Lott 100a.	220a.	2 - 1
JAMES JONES	Aberdeen	100a.	4 - 4
ELISHA JONES	Aberdeen	231a.	1 - 1

By William Richardson, assessor of PITTS CREEK 100

OWNERS NAME	LAND	TOTAL ACRES	White Inhab MALE-FEMALE
DANIEL JONES	none		2 - 3
MAJOR JONES	Winter Quarter	100a.	1 - 2
SOLOMON JOHNSON	Merrill Hall	60a.	3 - 2
WILLIAM LANE	Second Chance, Second Priviledge Locust Ridge Addn. and land from George Blake	700a.	2 - 2
FRANCIS LANE	none		4 - 5
ISAAC LAYFIELD	Hog Quarter 150a. Conveniency	300a.	7 - 7
CATEY LONG	none		3 - 3
SARAH LAMBDON	Chance	40a.	0 - 3
THOMAS LAMBDON	Chance	99a.	3 - 6
LITTLETON LONG	Long Acre 167a. Tylors Outlett 25a. Adventure 100a.	292a.	2 - 2
JESSE LONG	Piney Point	200a.	1 - 0
DAVID LONG	Piney Point	300a.	4 - 3
WALTER LANE	none		3 - 4
ABRAHAM LAMBERSON	Broad Ridge	50a.	2 - 1
LEVI LAMBERSON Jr.	Broad Ridge	50a.	0 - 0
SARAH LAMBERSON	none		0 - 2
WILLIAM LEWIS	none		2 - 4
JOHN MELTON	Security	75a.	1 - 2
JONATHAN MELVIN	Security	79a.	6 - 4
JOHN MELVIN	True Bridge & Winter Quarter	110a.	3 - 3
ROBERT MELVIN	Cowley	50a.	2 - 4
ALEXANDER MC CREDDY	Timber Grove	50a.	2 - 4
WILLIAM MERRILL	Merrils Addition Arracco, Long Trust 66a. Outlett 201a. Conviency 100a.	568a.	2 - 4
SCARBOROUGH MERRILL	Hog Ridge 30a. Security 301a. Hog Grove 22a. Arraco 6a. Merrils Discovery 14a. Merrills Delight 30a.	403a.	2 - 5
JOHN MILLS	Cherrystone	393a.	5 - 4
HUGH MILLS	Mills Security	200a.	1 - 4
SARAH MURRAY	none		0 - 3
BENJAMIN MILLS	Shanklins Lott	75a.	0 - 0
ROBERT MILLS	Shanklins, King Harrys Neck	289a.	3 - 3
GEORGE MELVIN Jr.	Cowley	50a.	4 - 5
DANIEL MAISON	none		3 - 4
DANIEL MIFFLIN	Mifflins Plrchase 665a. Meltons Purchase 70a.	735a.	0 - 0
SIMPSON MERRILL	none		5 - 6
LEVIN MERRIL (young man Simpson Merrill Security)			1 - 0
JOSEPH MERRILL Jr.	Arraco & Pittsborough	75a.	2 - 4
THOMAS MERRILL Jr.	Araco	161a.	1 - 4
JOHN MARSHALL	Cedar Hall	250a.	1 - 5
THOMAS MARSHALL	Conveniency & Rudder	244a.	4 - 2
WILLIAM MARSHALL	Keel 7a. Rudder 12a.	19a.	1 - 0
GEORGE MARSHALL (young man Thomas Marshall Sec.)			1 - 0
WILLIAM MELVIN	Cowley 100a. Golden Quarter	200a.	3 - 2
WILLIAM MELVIN Jr.	none		5 - 5
MARY MERRILL	Security	303a.	0 - 2
DANIEL MURRAY	none		2 - 1
SAMUEL McMASTERS	Double Purchase	230a.	2 - 2
SMITH MELVIN	Chestnut, Partnership & Champmans Adventure 40a.	270a.	0 - 0

By William Richardson, assessor of PITTS CREEK 100

OWNERS NAME	LAND	TOTAL ACRES	White Inhab. MALE - FEMALE
WILLIAM MILLS	Hill Glass 200a. pt. Aberdeen 53a. Pittsborrow 70a.	323a.	2 - 5
WILLIAM MILLS JR	(young man Wm.Mills Sr.Security)		1 - 0
SAMUEL MILLS	none		2 - 3
ELEANOR OKEY	none		2 - 4
RACHEL PRICE	Lloyds Lott	70a.	1 - 1
JAMES PHILLIPS	True Bridge	200a.	2 - 2
LEVIN POWELL	Piney Point	160a.	1 - 1
WILLIAM PEACOCK	none		4 - 4
JOHN PAYNE	Townsends Mistake & Smithfield	100a.	3 - 4
LEVI PILCHARD	none		2 - 2
HANNAH PARRADICE	none		0 - 3
SAMPSON PURKINS	(Mulatto.)		0 - 0
JAMES PATTERSON	Goodwill 300a. Leverton 225a. Mt. Pleasant 9a.	534a.	5 - 2
ROSANNA PARKS	none		0 - 1
MATTHEW PORTER	Meltons Purchase	75a.	3 - 3
JOHN PILCHARD	Mifflins Lott	100a.	2 - 4
DIXON QUINTON	Ledger 190a. Merrills Good will 35a. Last of All 259a. Orphans Swamp 100a. Partnership 13½a.	597½a.	2 - 0
NEHEMIAH REDDING	Aberdeen 102a. Dilaps 95a.	197a.	6 - 2
JOHN ROBINSON	none		3 - 3
STEPHEN ROACH	Fletchers Addition	100a.	0 - 0
PETER REDDING	Bratchers Purchase	150a.	2 - 1
BENJAMIN STEVENSON	Goshen	111a.	4 - 2
GEORGE STEVENSON	Goshen	205a.	2 - 0
JAMES STEVENSON	(young man)		1 - 0
JAMES SELBY	Double Purchase 214a. Piney Point 100a. Unknown 14a. ___? Ridges 50a.	478a.	3 - 2
ESTHER SMITH	Tully 245a. Mills Security	269a.	6 - 5
WILLIAM SMITH	(young man)		1 - 0
JOSEPH STEVENSON	Goshen	1075a.	3 - 2
JONATHAN STEVENSON	Goshen	1075a.	3 - 4
SAMUEL SMITH	none		1 - 5
JOSEPH SCHOOLFIELD	Desert 200a. Discovery 53a. Schoolfields Pleasure 155a.	408a.	5 - 5
HANNAH STERLIN	Cowley & Drown Cove 12a.	12a.	0 - 3
SOUTHY STERLING	Cowley	100a.	1 - 0
Melvin AYRES SMITH	none		1 - 3
ELIJAH TOWNSEND	Chapmans Choice 80a. Chapmans Adventue 20a. Refuge 7½a.	107½a.	3 - 5
JAMES TOWNSEND	none		2 - 5
WILLIAM TAYLOR	none		1 - 2
OBED TAYLOR	none		4 - 4
ANN TOWNSEND	none		3 - 4
PEGGY TAYLOR	none		0 - 2
JANETT TEAGUE	none		2 - 1
NEHEMIAH TINDALL	none		3 - 3
JAMES TINDALL	(young man Nehemiah Tindall Security)		1 - 0
THOMAS JEFFERSON TYLOR	Williams Desire	150a.	4 - 3

By Elisha Purnell assessor of QUEPONGO 100 (poor film)

OWNERS NAME	LAND	TOTAL ACRES	White Inhab. MALE-FEMALE
ISAAC AYRES	Murrays Industry 112a. Consolidation 104a.	216a.	0 - 0
WILLIAM ALLEN Sr.	Delight 130a. Tribulation?	229a.	0 - 0
SALIETHIEL BURBAGE	none		5 - 3
JETHRO BOWEN	Bowens Right 100a. Hogg Ridge 15a. Rounds Luck 30a. Bowens Luck 20a. Addition to Enlargment 73a. Jesamine 38a.	316a.	4 - 4
COMFORT BOWEN	Bownes Choice 51a. Thomas? Ridge 154a.	205a.	0 - 2
SOLOMON BRADFORD	Solomons Purchase 112a. Smith Hill 61a.	173a.	6 - 7
ELIAS BURBAGE	Landsdown 200a.	200a.	6 - 5
JOHN BASSETT	Timber Grove 100a. Branch Neck 100a.	200a.	2 - 1
WILLIAM BASSETT	none		2 - 4
GOERGE BLACK	none		3 - 3
WILLIAM BOWEN	Discovery	50a.	3 - 5
DAVID BOWEN	Hog Quarter	150a.	2 - 5
EDWARD BURBAGE	none		1 - 0
JESSE BOWEN	Sturbridge	7½a.	2 - 5
SARAH BOWEN	Hogsnorton	200a.	2 - 4
ELISHA BOWEN	none		0 - 0
JAMES BRADFORD	none		0 - 0
JOHN BURBAGE	Huntington 130a. Burbage Mistake 10a.	140a.	9 - 2
COMFORT BISHOP	Spittlefield	15a.	0 - 1
JEPTHAH NOWEN	none		1 - 1
MARTHAS?BURBAGE	none		0 - 4
ELIJAH BOWEN	none		0 - 0
JOHN BOWEN	none		0 - 0
LUKE BOWEN	St. Martins Ridge 60a. Addn. to Enjoymnet 60a. Bowens Discovery 24a.	144a.	3 - 5
MOSES CHAILLE	Lion Heath 350a. Long Lott 14a. Long Acre 55a. Addition 102a.	522a.	0 - 0
RACKLIFF BOWEN	none		0 - 0
LEVIN BOWEN	none		8 - 2
LEVI CRAPPER	Partnership 62½a. Addn. to ?	171a.	3 - 4
MAJOR CROPPER	none		0 - 0
CHAMBERS COLLINS	none		2 - 4
JOHN COLLINS	Purnells Security 50a. Hammond Adventure 29a. Rounds Outlett 104a.		3 - 2
JOHN DAVIS	Collickmore 243a. Bletchinghurst 7a. Mill Angle 56a. Jacob Bevans Chance 40a.	446a.	1 - 3
ESTHER COLLINS	Head of St.Lawrence Neck	140a.	0 - 1
WILLIAM CHRISTA	none		0 - 0
SOLOMON DAVIS	none		4 - 3
WILLIAM DAVIS	none		1 - 1
SOLOMON DAVIS	½ of Addition	63a.	3 - 9
THOMAS DUNCAN	Friends Choice	150a.	3 - 2
ISAAC DUNCAN	Friends Assistance Enlargment	100a.	3 - 2
JOHN DUBBERLY	none		1 - 0

By Elisha Purnell, assessor of QUEPONGO 100

OWNERS NAME	LAND	TOTAL ACRES	WHITE Inhab. MALE-FEMALE
LEVIN DUNCAN	Friends Assistance	140a.	4 - 2
SINAH DAVIS	none		1 - 1
BENJAMIN DAVIS	none		3 - 3
ELIZABETH EVANS	Golden Value	125a.	0 - 0
ELIZABETH ENNIS	Hog Range	80a.	1 - 3
COMFORT ELMORE	Spittlefield	248a.	2 - 2
GEORGE ENNIS	Gladstons Recovery 100a. Hudsons Beale 56a.	156a.	2 - 3
DAVID FITZGERAL	none		3 - 3
DAVID FASSITT	none		0 - 0
CHRISTOPHER GLASS	Hilliards Choice 158½a. Hills Mistake 23a.	181½a.	2 - 2
CHARLES GODFREY	West Chester	200a.	0 - 0
LEVIN GREEN	none		3 - 1
WILLIAM GRIFFIN	none		1 - 2
PATRICK GLASGOE	Brattans Choice 250a. Anne Down 330a. Mulberry Grove 250a. Enlargement 30a. Hazard 50a. Marthas Purchase 250a. Ditto 73a.	1893a.	3 - 2
LEVIN HILL	Robertsons Inheritance	106a.	4 - 4
JOHNSON HILL	Landsdown	195a.	2 - 3
WILLIAM HOLLAND	Landsdown	104a.	2 - 3
WILLIAM HAMMOND	Hammonds Adventure	84a.	5 - 5
JOSHUA HODGE	Williams? Contentment	84a.	1 - 0
JACOB HANCOCK	none		2 - 2
WHITTINGTON HANCOCK	none		0 - 0
ISAAC HAMMOND	none		1 - 5
MICHAEL HOLLAND	none		2 - 1
THOMAS HAMMOND	Jesemine 127a. Wakefield 50a. Sterbridge 8½a.	175½a.	5 - 6
WILLIAM HAMMOND Jr.	none		1 - 0
DENNIS HUDSON	Hudsons Beale	350a.	5 - 6
ISAAC HAMMOND	none		1 - 1
John? HOSHIER	none		0 - 0
HENRY HUDSON	St. Lawrance Marsh	66a.	4 - 3
ROBERT HUDSON	St. Lawrence	178a.	1 - 0
MARTHA HUDSON	St. Lawrence	88a.	2 - 2
UNITY? HUDSON	none		1 - 0
WILLIAM HUDSON	none		3 - 4
ESTHER HUDSON	St. Lawrence Neck	114a.	0 - 0
JESSE HUDSON	St. Lawrence	60½a.	1 - 2
LEVIN HENDERSON	Timbergrove	195a.	4 - 3
WILLIAM HOLLAND Jr.	Hollands Adventure 87a. Purnells Adventure 33a.	110a	2 - 3
JOHNSON JONES	Unity	102a.	4 - 5
THOMAS JONES	Winkfield	11 3/4a.	2 - 2
JOHN J. JONES	Richards Chance	100a.	2 - 6
WILLIAM JARMAN	Discovery	104a.	3 - 0
ELIJAH JARMAN	Bosworths Addition	60a.	1 - 0
WILLIAM JACKSON	none		2 - 2
GEORGE JONES	Thomas?? Luck	74a.	6 - 4

By Elisha Purnell, assessor of QUEPONGO 100

OWNERS NAME	LAND	TOTAL ACRES	White Inhab. MALE-FEMALE
JESSE JONES	Burbage Mistake 33 3/4a. Huntington 70a. Levin Heaths Addition 22½a.	126¼a.	5 - 2
MARY JOHNSON	none		2 - 2
EZEKIEL KNOX	Bosworth, Hunting Ridge	133½a.	1 - 2
SOLOMON LONG	name unknown	125a.	1 - 3
ELIZABETH LONG	Tukesberry	300a.	1 - 3
DAVID LONG	none		1 - 0
SAMUEL LONG	Brothers Security 435a. Newberry of Tukesberry 87a.	522a.	4 - 3
SOLOMON LONG	Asateague Fields, Charles Choice, ____ Lott & Addition to ___?	886a.	1 - 3
JESSE LONG	none		3 - 3
JOHN MORRIS	none		2 - 5
EDWARD MORRIS	Edwards Lott	71 3/4a.	2 - 2
ELIZABETH MORRIS	Sturbridge 27a.	27a.	2 - 1
NICHOLAS?MUMFORD	none		1 - 0
SAMUEL MARCHMENT	none		1 - 0
DAVID? MORRIS	none		1 - 0
JEPTHA MORRIS	none		1 - 0
CHARLES MARCHEMNT	none		5 - 3
WILLIAM MORRIS(Col.)	Collickmore 36a. Partnership 30a. Bletchinghurst 203a. Conviency 54a. (others.)	746a.	2 - 3
JOHN MARSHALL	St.Lawrence Neck 250a. Addition 102a. Liberty 50a. Conveniency 3½a. Hudsons Ruin 60a. Seabrant 24a.	599½a.	6 - 4
CORNELIUS MORRIS	none		2 - 1
THOMAS MUMFORD	none		2 - 1
CHARLES MUMFORD	Fellowship	79a.	2 - 3
LIFIELD MORRIS	Highfield	25a.	1 - 3
JOHN OUTTEN	Purnells Security	50a.	1 - 0
COMFORT OUTTEN	none		1 - 3
MATTHEW PURNELL Jr.	Williams Contention	104a.	4 - 3
JOHN PRIDDOX	Enlargement 80a. Burbage Mistake 26a. Gladstones Resurvey 10a.	116a.	2 - 3
LEVI PURNELL	Purnells Security 145a. Sherbern 138a. pt. Thomas P. Heirs 190a.	431a.	4 - 3
JOHN PURKINS	Spittlefield 235a. Deer Pasture 141a.	376a.	3 - 2
THOMAS POINTER	none		5 - 1
JOHN POINTER	none		1 - 2
ELIAS POINTER	Highfield	80a.	1 - 2
JOSEPH PORTER	Newberry 62a. Porters Addition? 222a.	284a.	1 - 0
COMFORT PORTER	none		0 - 4
PURNELL PORTER	Edwards Lott	100a.	4 - 1
ELIAS PENNIWELL	none		2 - 1
SARAH PURNELL	Purnells Security, Sherborn	300a.	0 - 4

By Elisha Purnell, assessor of QUEPONGO 100

OWNERS NAME	LAND	TOTAL ACRES	White Inhab. MALE-Female
MARY PURNELL	Baysend 200a. Jerico 200a. Crappers Neck 50a. Newberry 14a. Purnells Security 94a. Addition 15 3/4a.	573 3/4a.	2 - 1
BENJAMIN PURNELL	Purnells Security 150a.		0 - 0
MATTHEW PURNELL	Purnells Security 176a. Sherburn 100a. Purnells Industry 50a.	326a.	2 - 2
THOMAS PURNELL	Strife 203a. Hill Angle 43 3/4a. Purnells Purchase 164a. Harins? 50a.	450 3/4a.	2 - 0
ZADOCK PURNELL	Mill Angle 203½a. Strife	243½a.	2 - ?
JOHN PENNEWILL	none		2 - 2
ELIZABETH PURNELL	Strife 203½a. Golden Value 125a. Conclusion 120a. Mt. Hope 25a.	373½a.	0 - 1
THOMAS PURNELL	East Gate 463a. Lambertson Venture 29a. Timbergrove 100a. Br___? 850a.	1342a.	4 - 3
ELISHA PURNELL	Purnells Security 194a. Purnells Industry 10a. Addition 50a.	264a.	1 - 7
JAMES QUINTON	Collickmore & His Inheritance 206a. River Swamp 300a.	506a.	1 - 3
CHARLES RICHARDSON	Sherburn	100a.	2 - 3
JOHN RICHARD	Meddow (in his wifes Right)	114a.	1 - 1
MATTHEW RATCLIFFE	Husbands Torrent	300a.	2 - 3
JAMES RUARK	Lambertsons Venture	65a.	1 - 2
CHARLES RATCLIFFE	St. Lawrence 404a. Highfield 220a. Husbands Torrent 162a. Addition 23a. Liberty 24a.	833a.	6 - 3
SHADRACK RUARK	none		2 - 2
WHITTINGTON RICHARDSON	Bosworth	50a.	3 - 5
HAMMOND RENALDS	Winkfield	140½a.	3 - 2
JOHN ROUNDS	Johns Inheritance 420a. Collickmore 24a.	444a.	1 - 4
SAMUEL ROUNDS	Pitman, Poplar Ridge 96a.	251a.	0 - 0
Larence Rigsby	none		5 - 1
ISAAC RICHARDS	Batchelors Delight 50a. Addn. to Ditto 30a.	80a.	3 - 4
WILLIAM RICHARDS	none		1 - 0
WILLIAM RAIN	none		1 - 0
JOHN RACKLIFFE	Bowens Choice 200a. Deep Swamp 200a.	400a.	3 - 2
JOHN SMOCK	Security & Recovery 71a. Partnership 77a.	148a.	1 - 5
WILLIAM SELBY	Sandy Point & Addition 70a. pt. Ditto 167a. Timber Grove 61a.	298a.	5 - 2
ELIJAH SMITH	none		2 - 1
THOMAS SANDERS	Williams Contentment 100a.	100a.	2 - 2
JOHN SMITH	Highfield 97a. Blechinghurst	104a.	2 - 3

By Elisha Purnell, assessor of QUEPONGO 100

OWNERS NAME	LAND	TOTAL ACRES	White Inhab. MALE-FEMALE
JOHN SMOCK	Partnership	82½a.	3 - 4
RHODA SMOCK	Partnership 82½a.	82½a.	1 - 2
PARKER SELBY	Yorkshire 130a.	130a.	2 - 4
JAMES STEPHENS	none		1 - 0
Elijah Stephenson	none		1 - 0
Curtis? Stephenson	none		2 - 3
SARAH SMITH	Dukesberry 100a. Newbury 15a.	115a.	3 - 2
McKimmy SMOCK	Mt.Ephraim 197a. Matthews Lott	197a.	3 - 2
HOLLAND SMOCK	none		1 - 0
SAMUEL SMITH	Rachels Desire, Marbury & Marsh Grove & ?	326a.	3 - 2
DAVID TAYLOR	none		1 - 3
WILLIAM SMITH	Mulberry Grove 132a. and ? 200a.	332a.	4 - 1
JEREMIAH TOWNSEND	Desires Addnition	486a.	5 - 1
JOSEPH TAYLOR	Conveneincy	103a.	4 - 3
ELIZABETH THOMPSON	none		0 - 2
OUTTEN TRUITT	Mulberry Grove	90a.	4 - 3
LEVIN TOWNSEND	none		1 - 1
ELIAS TAYLOR	none		2 - 5
THOMAS TRUITT	none		4 - 3
JOHN WALKER	Conveniency	62a.	6 - 1
JAMES WILSON	Partnership 150a. Yorkshire	228a.	2 - 3
HENRY WHITE	Buckingham	150a.	2 - 4
JOHN WEBB	none		4 - 5
SUSANNAH? WEBB	none		2 - 3
SAMUEL WEBB	none		2 - 3

ACQUANGO 100

OWNERS NAME	LAND	TOTAL ACRES	White Inhab. MALE-FEMALE
GEORGE ATKINS	Partnership 150a.	150a.	2 - 1
JAMES ATKINSON	Choice	30a.	2 - 0
STEPHEN ATKINS	Hog Quarter 50a. Dear Harbour 167½a.	217½a.	3 - 5
MIDDLETON ATKINS	Dear Harbour 143a. Unknown 50a.	193a.	4 - 4
NIMROD ATKINS	Dear Harbour	20a.	1 - 1
Capt.WM.ALLEN	unknown	635a.	0 - 0
PEGGY ANDREWS	none		3 - 3
STEPHEN ADKINS Sr.	Dear Harbour	50a.	1 - 1
JOHN ADKINS	Forlorn Hope 67a. WOlfs Den 95a.	162a.	2 - 3
WILLIAM ADKINS	Forlorn Hope 33a. Dear Harbour 39a.	72a.	4 - 3
WINDER ADKINS	Dear Harbour 38½a.	38½a.	5 - 5
FASSITT BRUMBLY	none		3 - 2
THOMAS BEVANS Sr.	Pike 100a. Choice 100a. for Rowland Bevans 10a.	210a.	1 - 2
THOMAS BEVANS of Ch's	none		1 - 1
JESSE BRATTEN	none		0 - 0
BELITHA BRATTAN	none		5 - 4
JAMES BRATTAN	Turkey Ridge 42a. Black Soil 50a.	92a.	2 - 2

ACQUANGO 100

OWNERS NAME	LAND	TOTAL ACRES	White Inhab. MALE-FEMALE
WM. BETHARDS of Jarman	Addition to Inheritance 50a.	50a.	3 - 2
ELIZABETH BETHARDS	Addition to Inheritance	47½a.	0 - 5
Dr. SMITH BISHOP	Aquango 760a. Philadelphia	1060a.	2 - 4
SAMUEL BETHARDS	Tarkill Ridge 50a. Addn. to Inheritance 50a.	100a.	2 - 2
JOHN BRIDDLE (David Briddle Security)			0 - 0
DAVID BRIDDLE	Sandy Choice 30a. White Mountain 100a.	130a.	4 - 3
NATHANIEL BRITTINGHAM	none		1 - 1
LEVIN BLAKE	none		1 - 0
JOHN BASSITT of Wm.	Greenland 100a.	100a.	2 - 2
JOHN NICHOLSON	Peters Chance 20a. Poplar Ridge 60a. Bought of Thomas Johnson 55a.	135a.	2 - 6
JAMES NAIRNE	Northfield	195a.	0 - 0
LEVIN NOBLE	none		1 - 1
SABROUGHNOBLE	none		0 - 0
MATHIAS OUTTEN	PittRidges	100a.	2 - 3
LEVI OUTTEN	same bou/o Mr. Johnson	160a.	2 - 0
MOSES PAYNE	Addition 100a. Woodyard	150a.	8 - 2
WILLIAM PORTER	Partnership	50a.	2 - 3
HENRY PARKER Jr.	Wickenou Neck 22a. Shingle Point 9a. Middlemore 18a. Birth 57a.	106a.	0 - 0
WILLIAM PARKER	Wickenou Neck 66a. Shingle Point 9a.	75a.	0 - 0
PARKER SCHOOLFIELD	Wickenos Neck	112a.	4 - 1
THOMAS PARKER	none		0 - 0
GABRIEL POWELL Jr.	none		1 - 3
ZADOCK POWELL	none		0 - 0
WILLIAM POWELL	none		1 - 2
SELBY PARKER	Armenia	210a.	2 - 7
ZADOCK PURNELL	Land of Mrs. Anderson 230a. Swamp Lands 450a.	680a.	0 - 0
THOMAS POWELL	Strife	50a.	2 - 4
ELISHA PENNEWEILL	none		2 - 2
RICHARD POUNDERS	Fountains Choice	52a.	1 - 2
RICHARD PENNEWEILL	none		2 - 3
GEORGE PENNEWELL	unknown	50a.	0 - 0
MARGARET PENNEWELL	widow of Thomas, Pennewells Purchase 100a.		1 - 5
KIMMEY? PENNEWELL	none		6 - 5
GABRIEL POWELL	Powells Neck 50a. Gabriels Purchase 100a.	150a.	3 - 2
JOHN PENNEWELL	none		3 - 1
HENRY PARKER Sr.	Wrixoms Purchase 115a. Long Ridge 50a. Eshoms Choice 32a.	197a.	5 - 5
JOHN PARKER of Henry,	none		0 - 0
JOHN PARKER of Chas.	none		2 - 2
CHARLES PARKER	Armenia	210a.	2 - 6
SCARBROUGH PARKER	Parkers Adventure	231½a.	2 - 4
JOHN PARSONS Sr.	Addn. to Parsons Lott 206a. TarrHill Ridge 50a. Tyborn Hill 50a. Parsons Island 40a.	396a.	4 - 7

ACQUANGO 100

OWNERS NAME	LAND	TOTAL ACRES	White Inhab. MALE-FEMALE
ZEPHANIAH PARSONS	Egg Point	50a.	4 - 4
SWICY POINTER	none		0 - 0
JOHN PARSONS	Addnition to Inheritance	80a.	0 - 0
PORTER PARSONS	unknown	44a.	1 - 2
BARTHOLOMEW SLAUGHTER	Bartholomews First Attempt.	259a.	0 - 0
MARK SCOTT	none		1 - 2
THOMAS SCOTT	none		1 - 2
THOMAS TRUITT of Littleton,	none		2 - 1
JOHN TOWNSEND	Wolf Pitt Ridge	143a.	4 - 4
	Townsends Purchase	47a.	
GEORGE TURNER	Choice	134a.	1 - 0
THEOPHILUS TURNER	Forrest Of MarySherwood	154a.	2 - 4
LEVIN TOWNSEND	none		1 - 2
JOSHUA TOWNSEND	Carolina 100a. Parkers Adventure 160½a.	260½a.	0 - 0
LITTLETON TRUITT	Truitts Lott		2 - 3
THOMAS TYRE	none		4 - 4
GEORGE TRUITT	none		3 - 1
JOB TRUITT	Hardship 356a. Addition to Red Oak Ridge, Williams Folly 37a. Drum? Choice 101a. Passing Hill 50a.	985a.	1 - 6
GEORGE TRUITT of Job.	Parsons Addition 46a. Maple Toss 60a.	106a.	1 - 0
ZADOCK TURNER (Thomas Nlizzard Security)	none		0 - 0
WILLIAM TWILLEY	Coxes Chance 60a. Phillips Strife 61a.	121a.	3 - 4
ELIJAH TINDALL	Discovery 50a. Chance Increase 50a. Lebonte?? 50a.	150a.	2 - 1
ELISHA TIMMONS	none		2 - 3
JAMES TIMMONS	Partnership 20a. Long Ridge 35a.	55a.	2 - 4
WHITTINGTON TIMMONS	Long Ridge	15a.	0 - 0
WILLIAM TIMMONS	Harris Outlett	50a.	3 - 2
NEHEMIAH TIMMONS	Hog Quarter	50a.	5 - 3
EBENEZER TRUITT	none		1 - 1
LEVI TIMMONS	Swains Adventure	40a.	1 - 5
JAMES TRUITT	none		4 - 3
CALEB TINGLE	unknown	300a.	0 - 0
SAMUEL TIMMONS	none		3 - 5
JOHN TRUITT for John Gadies heirs-	Davis Choice 70a. Peeches Ridge 10a. Hog Pen Ridge 50a. Davis Choice Enlarged(for self)	327a.	3 - 4
ELI TARR	Wickenos Neck	100a.	3 - 3
SARAH TURNER w/o Henry-	Henrys Ridge, Fiddlers Lott 25a.)	50a.	3 - 1
ELISHA VINSON	none		1 - 3
WILLIAM DAVIS	none		1 - 1
JOSHUA DAVIS	Davis Chance 22a. Long Ridge 163a. Davis Chance 64a. Hog Quarter 20a.	169a.	5 - 4
SAMUEL DAVIS	Wild Cat Ridge 22½a. Hickory Ridge 27a. Bou/o Capt. Dashiell 93a.	132½a.	3 - 4

ACQUANGO 100

OWNERS NAME	LAND	TOTAL ACRES	White Inhab MALE-FEMALE
BENJAMIN DAVIS	Hogg Down	130a.	1 - 1
JEMAS DAVIS	Hog Down	150a.	4 - 2
THOMAS DAVIS	Davis Chance 72a. Adventure 50a. End of Dispute 32a.	154a.	1 - 3
PHILLIP DAVIS	Phillips Luck 25a. Brumbleys Purchase 112a. Same bou/o Dashiell 112a. Hog Quarter 21a.	270a.	3 - 4
ANN DAVIS-widow	Pig Pen Ridge 40a. Adventure 104a.	144a.	2 - 3
NIXON DAVIS	Adventure 144a.		1 - 2
SHADRACK DAVIS	none		1 - 3
THOMAS DONOVAN	none		1 - 3
ZEDEKIAH DAVIS	none		3 - 3
ROBERT DAVIS	Davis Choice	112a.	2 - 3
JOHN DAVIS of John	none		0 - 0
LEVIN DUNCAN Jr.	Duncans Lelight	250a.	0 - 0
LEVIN DUNCAN of Chas.	none		3 - 5
CHARLES DUNCAN	Addn. to Charles Lott 135a. Troys Discovery 50s. Hog Hill 50a.	235a.	0 - 0
MATTHEW DALE	Givans Chance 113a. End of Dispite 100a.	213a.	0 - 0
JAMES DALE	Hog Quarter 130a.	130a.	0 - 0
JOHN DAVIS of Hill	End of Dispute 372a. Hog Quarter 50a. Chance 30a. Condomim 10a. Ryleys Portion 191a. Johnsons Industry 90a.	743a.	1 - 2
WILLIAM DENNIS Sr.	Hardship	75a.	5 - 5
JOHN DENNIS	(Wm. Dennis Security) none		0 - 0
JOSIAH DENNIS	Colliers Delight	150a.	0 - 0
JOSHUA DENNIS	none		4 - 3
JAMES DENNIS	(Johnson Dennis Security)		0 - 0
HENRY DENNIS	(Johnson Dennis Security)		0 - 0
MATHIAS DENNIS	(Johnson Dennis Security)		0 - 0
THOMAS DALE	Colliers Delight	522a.	0 - 0
WILLIAM DRADDON	none		0 - 0
ISAAC DREADON	none		3 - 3
MARTHA PARSONS	Cabin Ridge	15a.	3 - 1
ABRAM POLLITT	none		0 - 0
JOSIAH ROBINS	Greenland 139a. Addition to Greenland 50a.		6 - 3
DANIEL RUARK	none		1 - 2
JOSEPH RICHARDSON	Partnership	25a.	2 - 0
SAMUEL RICHARDSON	Partnership	68a.	0 - 0
WILLIAM RICHARDSON	Sr. Partnership	25a.	2 - 3
MATTHEW RICHARDSON	Partnership	30a.	3 - 4
JOHN RACKLIFFE	none		0 - 0
LITTLETON ROBINS	Addition to Long Delay 130a. Long Delay 125a. Forrest Range 110a.	385a.	0 - 0
NEHEMIAH ROBBINS	none		4 - 2

ACQUANGO 100

OWNERS NAME	LAND	TOTAL ACRES	White Inhab. MALE-FEMALE
JOHN REED	End of Dispute	75a.	2 - 6
WILLIAM ROUND	Forrest Range	206a.	6 - 3
WHITTINGTON RICHARDSON	none		0 - 0
THOMAS ROBINSON(Mulatto)	Phillips Adventure	100a.	0 - 0
JOHN RAIN	TarrKill Ridge 50a. Bee Hive Ridge 50a. Greenland 100a.	200a.	1 - 3
WILLIAM ROBERTS	Roberts Choice	190a.	1 - 4
ARMLAUTER?ROBINS	none		0 - 0
WILLIAM SMITH	DUNCANS DELIGHT 52a. Roberts Choice 25a.	78a.	0 - 0
McKIMMY SMOCK	Smocks Land	167a.	0 - 0
WILLIAM SELBY OF JOHN	none		2 - 1
NIXON SELBY	Choice	140a.	1 - 2
JACOB STURGIS	Jacobs Lott 50a. Friends Assistance 50a.	100a.	1 - 3
SOLOMON SHOCKLEY	Shockleys Choice 100a. Greenfield 100a.	200a.	2 - 0
GEORGE SMITH	(Job Truitt Security) none		1 - 0
JOHN SHOCKLEY	none		0 - 0
DANIEL SELBY	none		0 - 0
RICHARD SHOCKLEY Sr.	Shockleys Choice	267a.	2 - 2
RICHARD SHOCKLEY Jr.	Shockleys Choice	90a.	4 - 4
WILLIAM SHOCKLEY	Shockleys Choice	50a.	3 - 2
BENJAMIN SHOCKLEY of Jon.	Pittsburg 50a. Buck Ridge 15a.	65a.	4 - 2
WILLIAM SPEAR	Spears Adventure 50a. Gillis Rich Ground 20a. unknown 202a.	272a.	5 - 1
HENRY SPEAR	Cherry Garden	43a.	1 - 4
BENJAMIN SHOCKLEY Sr.	Tilghmans Goodwill 25a. Fountains Choice 176a. Pilchards Island ??	221a.+	5 - 4
TRUITT BRITTINGHAM	Brittinghams Fortune 20a. Bartholomews First Attempt.	20a. 31a.	1 - 4
WILLIAM BASSITT	Bassetts Choice 13a. Unknown 227a.	227a.	1 - 3
John??BRITTINGHAM of Nathaniel-	Potatoe Swamp 13 3/4a. Hoggdown 24a. Ryleys Portion 9a. Brittinghams Choice 34a.	$80\frac{3}{4}$a.	2 - 4
HENRY BRUMBLY	none		2 - 5
JOHN BRITTINGHAM	Truitts Choice	$73\frac{1}{2}$a.	4 - 2
ISIAH BRIDDLE	none		3 - 5
JOHN BRATTEN	none		5 - 5
SOLOMON BAKER	none		2 - 1
WILLIAM BRITTINGHAM of Pocomoke-	none		3 - 3
ROBERT BITTS	Wickenos Neck	100a.	0 - 0
SOLOMON BAKER	Gargotha 50a. Black Soil 70a.	120a.	3 - 2
LEVIN BAKER of Solomon-	none		0 - 0
LEAH BLIZZARD widow	none		1 - 2
THOMAS BLIZZARD	Friendship	73a.	2 - 2
RACKLIFFE BLIZZARD	Hog yard	50a.	3 - 5
LITTLETON BEAUCHAMP	none		1 - 2
JOSEPH BRITTINGHAM of Jas.	Chance	50a.	4 - 3

ACQUANGO 100

OWNERS NAME	LAND	TOTAL ACRES	White Inhab. MALE-FEMALE
JOSEPH BENSON	Colliers Delight	200a.	2 - 3
JOHN PARSONS BLIZZARD	Addn. to Parsons Lott	40a.	3 - 1
BENJAMIN BISHOP	Buck Ridge	50a.	1 - 1
WILLIAM BETHARDS of Wm.	Dogwood Ridge	50a.	5 - 5
PETER CHAILLE	Col. Goshen 600a. Nelsons Security 93a. Johnsons Venture 70a. Whittingtons Choice 23a. Peters Chance 115a. Williams Choice 29a.	930a.	5 - 6
JOHN CORDREY	Addn. to Broad Neck 100a. Hog Quarter 80a.	186½a.	4 - 3
HENRY CORKWELL	(Wm. Farlow Security)		4 - 2
JOHN CAMPBELL	none		1 - 1
RACHEL CUTLER	Golden Mine	35a.	2 - 2
MOSES CHAILLE	none		4 - 2
EZEKIEL CLAYWILL	Farlows Survey	210a.	0 - 0
MAJOR CLAYWILL	none		5 - 5
THOMAS COTTINGHAM Sr.	Cottinghams Choice 100a. Cottinghams Second Choice	145a.	3 - 3
WILLIAM CAMBRIDGE (Mulatto)	Williams Choice Enlarged 49a.	49a.	0 - 0
TRUITT DAVIS	Hoggs down	100a.	4 - 3
JAMES DOWNES	name unknown	100a.	0 - 0
JOHN GILES	Davis Adventage 136a. Trible Purchase 66a.	202a.	3 - 4
CHRISTOPHER GLASS	For McKimmy Smock-	153a.	0 - 0
JOHN HUDSON	Choice	66a.	2 - 3
WILLIAM HANDY of Thomas,	name unknown	204a.	0 - 0
MADUX HAMBLEN	Bear Harbour	48a.	3 - 3
BENJAMIN HAMBLIN	New Castle	150a.	0 - 0
EBENEZER HERON (of Sussex)	Gillis Richland	50a.	0 - 0
JONATHAN HERON for G. Farlow	Buckridge	74a.	0 - 0
JAMES HEATH	Hickory Neck	50a.	2 - 2
JOSEPH HOLLOWAY	Dear Harbour	100a.	1 - 1
HANNAH HEATH	none		0 - 3
SARAH HAYWARD, widow	Leeds 623a. Second Addition 87a. Wing 100a.	800a.	1 - 3
CATHERINE HALL	none		0 - 1
EZEKIEL HOZIER	none		1 - 0
Capt. WM. HANDY	Double Purchase 246a. Armenia 20a. Gloucester 58a. Whittingtons Meadow 30a. Castle Green 150a. Causeys Place 180a. Kings Necessity & Kings Addition 179a.	863a.	7 - 2
SHADRACK HADDER	none		1 - 5
LAVINA HOZIER	Forrest Grove	40a.	3 - 4
JOHN HOZIER	Pennewills Choice 40a. Hoziers Security 1a.	41a.	0 - 0
JAMES HOUSTON	Houstons Chance	121a.	0 - 0
ISAAC HOUSTON (land for Sturgis Heirs)	Sturgis Addn. to Timothys Point 95a. Wickones Neck 500a. Castle Green 133¼a. Trible Purchase 74a. Murrays Loss 220a. Batchelors Delight 50a. Neiborours Mistake 112a.	1184a.	5 - 4

ACQUANGO 100

OWNERS NAME	LAND	TOTAL ACRES	White Inhab. MALE-FEMALE
WILLIAM HAMMOND	Flattland 100a. Strife 100a.	200a.	0 - 0
WILLIAM HOZIER	Truitts Goodwill 100a. Hoziers Addition 18a.	118a.	4 - 4
CURTIS HENDERSON	none		1 - 1
WILLIAM JARMAN	none		5 - 3
GILES JONES OF Wm.	none		0 - 0
JOHN JONES OF Wm.	none		0 - 0
JAMES JARMAN	Ninepin Neck 50a. Addition 25a. Hickory Point 22a.	97a.	4 - 5
OBED JONES	Hog Quarter	75a.	0 - 0
ELISHA JONES	none	75a.	2 - 1
WILLIAM JONES of John	Hog Quarter	100a.	3 - 1
WILLIAM JONES	unreadable 78 & 32a.	110a.	3 - 5
SAMUEL DREADON	Chailes Neck 50a. Addition to Chailles Neck 78a.	128a.	5 - 1
WILLIAM DICKERSON	Taylors Sandy Field 96a. Dickersons Venture 33a. Crooked Lane 32a.	161a.	4 - 4
VALENTINE DENNIS	Security	125a.	1 - 2
BENJAMIN DENNIS	Partnership 3a. Bald Cyrpress 25a. Choice 52a. Golden Mine 71a.	151a.	3 - 4
ANNANIAS DAVIS	Partnership	106a.	0 - 0
JOHN DENNIS of Johnson,	none		1 - 1
JOHNSON DENNIS	Bassitts Choice 84a. Hickory Point 64a.	148a.	8 - 4
WILLIAM DENNIS of Johnson,	none		1 - 1
JOHN DAVIS	unreadable	50a.	4 - 5
HENRY DENNIS	land in Indian town	625a.	0 - 0
JOSEPH ENNIS Jr.	none		0 - 0
JONATHAN ESHUM	Hickory Hill	12a.	5 - 1
JACOB EVANS	name lost	30a.	1 - 5
BENJAMIN FARLOW	Benjamins Choice	50a.	2 - 1
WILLIAM FARLOW	Dikes Folly	120a.	5 - 2
JONATHAN FOOKS	Addition to Philadelphia	400a.	3 - 2
JOHN FARLOW	Mulling Field	202a.	6 - 2
STEPHEN FOUNTAIN	White Mountain	100a.	
DANIEL FOOKS	Tower Hill 96a. Philadelphia 50a. Hog Yard 125a. Poplar Neck 50a. Fair?Land 101a. Conclusion 14a.	436a.	7 - 0
JOHN GIVAN	Hogs Down 22a. Advenure 100a.	122a.	3 - 0
ROBERT GIVAN	Adventure 30 3/4a.	30 3/4a.	1 - 0
GOERGE GIVAN For Jacob Reeds Heirs.	Jacobs Cohiers 260a. End of Dispute 6a. Hickory Point 26½a. Saplen Neck 100a.	392½a.	3 - 5
ROUND GIVAN	Givans Chance 200a. land for John Fassitt? 150a.	350a.	4 - 5
sarah gray	none		1 - 2
OLIVER GIRFFIN	Griffins Chance	180a.	2 - 1
JOHN GRIFFIN	Happy Entrance 40a. Unknown	99a.	2 - 3
ALEXANDER GIVAN	none		2 - 4
CHARLES GODFREY	Godfreys Security 250a. Godfreys Surprise 56a.	306a.	1 - 2
LEVIN GODFREY	none		0 - 0

ACQUANGO 100

OWNERS NAME	LAND	TOTAL ACRES	White Inhab. MALE-FEMALE
JAMES GODFREY	Williams Lott 150a. Godfreys Chance 100a. ___? 27a.	277a.	4 - 0
JAMES VICTOR	none		1 - 2
THOMAS VICTOR Jr.	none		1 - 2
JOHN VICTOR	Black Soil	259a.	2 - 5
THOMAS VICTOR Sr.	Victors Addition 121a. Victors Industry 70a. Pzrtnership 15½a. Puzzle for ___? 15½a.	222a.	1 - 2
BATHSHEBA WINDSOR	Nohe		0 - 1
SARAH WHITE	none		1 - 1
BARKLEY WHITE	Kingsdale 100a. For Wm. Johnson 40a.	140a.	3 - 2
THOMAS WHITE	Whites Industry	74a.	2 - 1
ELIAS WEBB	none		4 - 2
ISAAC WILKINS	none		1 - 4
JOSHUA WHITE	none		0 - 0
WILLIAM WHITE	Philadelphia	100a.	3 - 2
GROVER WOODLY	none		2 - 3
MAJOR WILKINS	none		3 - 3
ZEPHANIAH WEBB	none		2 - 3
JAMES WARD	Contented Batchelors Lott 50a. Piney Neck 150a.	200a.	3 - 3
JOHN WHITE	Houstons Lott 50a. Silver Stream 30a. Constantinople	180a.	3 - 2
ABIEL WRIGHT	none		5 - 3
ELIJAH WILLIS	none		0 - 0
JEPTHA WEBB	Duncans Delight	50a.	3 - 2
JESSE WILLIAMS	Ivy Neck	100a.	2 - 4
ELISHA WHEELOR	Duncans Delight 100a. Enlarged	100a.	3 - 3
ELIZABETH WINNS	none		0 - 0
WILLIAM TURNER	Newfoundland	75a.	4 - 3
BARKLEY TOWNSEND	Forrist Grove 148a. Barkleys Addition 7a. Townsends Adventure 54a.	209a.	4 - 4
SAMUEL TRUITT Jr.	none		1 - 1
JOHN TRUITT Sr.	Cally Swamp	30a.	5 - 1
JEREMIAH TOWNSEND	none		0 - 0
ZEDEKIAH TRUITT	none		0 - 0
GEORGE TRUITT	none		0 - 0
HENRY KILEY	none		5 - 2
CHARLES KILEY	none		1 - 2
MARY LOWRY, widow	Good Hopes	79a.	4 - 4
WILLIAM LEWIS	Pleasant Grove 50a. Forrest Range 250a.	300a.	5 - 3
GEORGE LEWIS	Long Delay 40a. Brown Dam Ridge 30a.	70a.	1 - 3
JAMES LEWIS	Jarmans Chance 50a.	50a.	5 - 3
THOMAS LEWIS	none		1 - 1
ARTHUR LEWIS	Land of Promise	50a.	3 - 5
LEVI LAMBERSON	none		0 - 0
ELIJAH LAWS Sr.	Laws Second Addition 218a. Little Neck 21a.	239a.	1 - 3
JOSHUA LAWS	Laws Second Addition 146a. Laws Outlett 98a.	244a.	1 - 1
ELIJAH LAWS Jr.	Laws Outlett 98a. Addn. to Hog Quarter 146a. Outletts Addn. 280a.		2 - 2

ACQUANGO 100

OWNERS NAME	LAND	TOTAL ACRES	White Inhab. MALE-FEMALE
WILLIAM LAWS	Laws Addition 116a. Strifes survey 40a.	156a.	2 - 2
WILLIAM MORRIS	Cabbin Neck 115a. Fountains Choice 65½a. Shingle Point 20a.	200½a.	5 - 4
SAMUEL MAGEE	name unknown	60a.	1 - 3
TURVILL MUMFORD	none		2 - 1
BENNETT MAISON	none		4 - 2
JOHN McDANIEL	McDaniels Purchase	113a.	3 - 4
JOHN MUMFORD	Cumberland 150a. Laws Second Choice 65a. Cypress Savanah 63a.	278a.	2 - 1
JAMES MUMFORD Jr.	Struggle	158a.	1 - 1
JAMES MUMFORD Sr.	Mumfords Adventure Enlarged 278a. Mumfords Folly 7a. Myrtle berry Gorve 75a. Abishas Hardship 57a.	417a.	2 - 2
ABISHA MUMFORD	(Jas.Mumford Security)none		0 - 0
JOHN MITCHELL	Little Neck Enlarged 291a. Golden Value 800a. Aydelots Beaver Dam 125a.	1217a.	5 - 2
JOSIAH MITCHELL	Hog yard	170a.	0 - 0
SARAH MUMFORD	none		0 - 1
JAMES MITCHELL	Beach Ridge & Quoaquson	200a.	0 - 0
JAMES MURRAY of Annapolis, Doctor, unknown		1179a.	0 - 0
JOHN MITCHELL	none	25a.	1 - 1
THOMAS McCLISH Jr.	Tower Hill	50a.	3 - 3
THOMAS MARTIN, C apt.	Selbys Security 250a. Acquantico Savanah 82a. Addn. to Selbys Security 38a. Killams Choice 123a. Partnership 55a.	448a.	5 - 3

	BUCKINGHAM 100	ACRES	White Inhab.
WILLIAM ALLISON	none		0
HOWARD AYDELOTTE	New Addition, Howards Content Addition to New Addition	385a.	8
WILLIAM AKE	Hog Quarter	100a.	
JOHN AYDELOTTE	none		
MARY AYDELOTTE	Miserable Quarter	109a.	
MARY ARDIS	Addition to Friends Discovery	50a.	
LUKE ATKINSON	none		3
CHARLES BANNISTER	Purkins Venture 82a. Emits Discovery 33 1/3a. Tanlon 100a.	215 1/3a.	3
ELISHA BRADFORD	none		4
ISAAC BRITTINGHAM	none		
TABITHA BAYLEY	unknown	50a.	
WILLIAM BOWEN	Emmits Discovery 33½a.	33½a.	
THOMAS BATSON	Powells Lott	25a.	
WILLIAMBRASURE	none		
JOHN BREVARD	Polks Neglect 295a. Friendship 120a. Moutn Hope 225a. Long Ridge 100a. Essex 80a.	820a.	

ACQUANGO 100

OWNERS NAME	LAND	TOTAL ACRES	WHITE INHAB.
BELITHA BRASURE	none		4
ELIHU BRIDDLE	Mt.Pleasant 100a. Mt. Hope 34a. Long Ridge 150a. unknown 150a. Long Trust 65a. Cornils ? Swamp 5a.	586a.	
JOHN BEAUCHAM	Saw Mill Range	150a.	7
WILLIAM BRADFORD	none		6
MARY BRAVARD	none		
WILLIAM BAKER	none		
ZADOCK BAKER	none		
ARCHIBALD BAKER	none		
GEORGE BAKER	Whaleys Venture 50a.		
SALATHIEL BAKER	none		4
PETER COLLIER	none		2
WILLIAM COLLIER	Slaughter Ridge 200a.	200a.	8
NATHANIEL CROPPER	Sr. Crappers Discovery	200a.	8
COMFORT COLLIER	Burly 100a. Enlargement 110a.	210a.	
SOLOMON CAMPBELL	none		6
LEVI CROPPER	none		7
HANNAH CROPPER	none		1
SOLOMON COLLINS	none		10
SOLOMON CAREY	none		
WILLIAM COFFIN	none		2
EBENEZER CAMPBELL	Cumberland 160a. Brotherhood 348a.	408a.	0
SARAH COLLIER	Carmell	883a.	5
JOSEPH CURLIS	Golden Quarter	235a.	4
WILLIAM CAMPBELL	none		6
ADEN CURLIS	none		2
BENJAMIN CLARK	none		4
EPHRAIM CAHOON	none		4
BENJAMIN CURLIS	none		2
JAMES CROPPER	none		3
LYDIA CLARK (of Garshon)	none		4
WILLIAM COLLINS(of Price)	none		1
WILLIAM COLLIER	none		6
THOMAS DALE	Redland Enlarged	150a.	9
JOSIAH DALE	Mt. Pleasant, Luck in Time, Hard Luck, Chance & Slipe, Second Additon, Powells Purchase Slipe	759a.	10
ABIJAH DAVIS	Calebs Discovery 14a. Friendship 29a. Friends Advice 120a.	163a.	7
JESSEE DAVIS	Last Choice 105a. Partnership 22½a. Bear Quarter & Hamblins Folly 310a.	457a.	11
SAMUEL DALE	Castle Hill	66½a.	3
JOHN DALE	Bear Quarter 90a. Castle Hill 100a. Luck in Time 60a. Castle Low 16a. Luck in Time 15a.	28a.	7
JAMES DALIFFOUNT	none		6
JAMES DAVIS	none		4
LEVI DAVIS	none		5
MATTHEW DALE	Welch Tract	43a.	1

BUCKINGHAM 100

OWNERS NAME	LAND	TOTAL ACRES	WHITE INHAB.
JAMES DALE	Welch Tract	260a.	6
MATHIAS DAVIS	Friends Advise 174a. Addn. to Richardsons Ridge 70a.	244a.	7
EDWARD DAVIS	none		8
JOHN DIOR	none		0
LEVI FALL	Northampton	141a.	3
William Falkinor	none		1
AMUTA FRANKLIN	Security	200a.	5
ELIJAH FASSITT	Fishing Harbour 25a. Nathan Choice 250a. Ditto 100a. Bredwell 50a. 2nd. Adventure 36a.	661a.	0
DAVID FASSITT	Cornwell 500a. Of W.P. 50a. Hill Hall 160a. Addition & Venture 82a. Pinders Neglect & Chance. Of Steward 500a.	1442a.	7
WILLIAM GAULT	Franklins Security	25a.	6
BENJAMIN GRAY	Security Enlarged 64a. Conclusion 54a.	118a.	9
THOMAS GRAY Jr.	Grays Lott Enlarged 160a. Bacon Quarter 60a. Grays Lott 30a.	240a.	7
JOSEPH GRAY	Security Enlarged 106a. Grays Lott Enlarged 25a. Ditto 27a. Security Enlarged 43a.	201a.	7
JESSE GRAY	Bacon Quarter 35a. Conclusion 217a. Grays Chance 40a. Long Tryall 2 3/4a.	$314\frac{3}{4}$a.	8
THOMAS GRAY Sr.	Grays Lott Enlarged	146a.	3
JOHNSON GRAY	DUKES HILL 100a. Secrutity Enlarged 81a. Grays Lott Enlarged 100a.	281a.	1
JEDIAH GRAY	Grays Lott	130a.	7
BELITHA GRIFFIN	Sands	100a.	5
ARCHIBALD GAULT	Obeds Wilderness	26a.	5
THOMAS GREER	Farwells Addition 40a. Farwells Folly 64a. Farwells Venture 6a.	110a.	1
ISAAC GRAY	none		5
WILLIAM GRAY Sr.	none		2
JOSEPH GODFREY	Hog Quarter, Brandy Hill, Addn. to New Addition	150a.	6
REBECCA HILL	Neighborhood	400a.	2
STEPHEN HILL	Neighborhood	300a.	5
ELISHA HOLLOWAY	Archibalds Discovery 257a. Crooked Lane 135a.	392a.	5
HENRY HANCOCK	Castle Hill	50a.	8
SAMUEL HOLLAND Jr.	Bacon Quarter 190a. Well Joined 83a. Oak Hall 48a. Neglect 34a.	354a.	1

YOUNG MEN

ERASMAS HARRISON (Erasmas Harrison Security
JONATHAN CAREY
SOLOMAN GUNDY
JACOB HOLLOWAY

BUCKINGHAM 100

OWNERS NAME	LAND	TOTAL ACRES	WHITE INHAB.
YOUNG MEN			
BENJAMIN GRAY (Benjamin Gray Security)			
JESSE DALE (John DALE Security)			
LOUDON CROPPER (Jno.C. Cropper Security)			
LEVIN CROPPER (John C. Cropper Security)			
BELITHA TOWNSEND			
CHARLES GODFREY (Joseph Godfrey Security)			
ELISHA WEBB			
GODFREY BRASHIER			
WILLIAM BRASHURE			
KENDALL PATEY (Powell Patey Security)			
WILLIAM COVINGTON			
DAVID GRAY			
WILLIAM GRAY ofWm.			
JOSEPH HOLLOWAY (thomas Holloway Security)			
JOHN SMITH (Belitha Griffin Security)			
JOHN HENDERSON			
MILBY SMITH (John Smith Security)			
ELIJAH TIMMONS (Elijah Timmons Security)			
ISAAC PURNELL			
JOSHUA MITCHELL Jr.			
ROBERT MITCHELL			
LEVIN MITCHELL			
THOMAS DAVIS			
JOHN HILL			
JOSEPH GREEN			
LABAN TAYLOR			
SAMUEL TAYLOR Jr.			
ALEXANDER TAYLOR			
THOMAS HUDSON			
BENJAMIN HUDSON			
WILLIAM WYATT (S.H.Round Security)			
WILLIAM WATERS			
JOHN JUSTICE			
ANN^S POWELL			
JESSEE POWELL			
PETER PURNELL			
STEPHEN TAYLOR			
ISAAC LYNCH			
JAMES BRITTINGHAM			
ROUSE HARRISON			
WILLIAM RYAN			
BENJAMIN TIMMONS (Levin Timmons Security)			
JAMES BASSITT	none		3
HEZEKIAH BEVANS	none		5
JESSEE CROPPER	none		6
JONATHAN CORDREY	Adventure, Addition to Wharton 100a.	100a.	0
SOLO. HAMBLEN	none		2
TABITHA COLLIER	Batchelors Hall	100a.	3
ABISHA DAVIS	none		1
WILLIAM MOORE	none		2
AARON WILSON	none		3

BUCKINGHAM 100

OWNERS NAME	LAND	TOTAL ACRES	White Inhab.
WILLIAM WHITTINGTON Jr.	Timber Choice	700a.	0
COL. JOHN DENNIS	Fragment 360a. Showells Addition 16a. Cornhill conclusion 52a. Holloway Point 30a.	474a.	0
WILLIAM PURNELL of John	unknown 700a. Grist Mill 50a.	750a.	0
ANDRIA STUART	none		0
JOSEPH TAYLOR	none		6
ISRAEL TOWNSEND	Temple Hall 233a. Puzzle & Plague 100a.	333a.	5
CHARLES TAYLOR	Thomas's Hall	110a.	0
JOHN TULL	Friends Assistance 210a. Saw Mill Range 760a. Miserable Quarter 37a. Winter Range 50a.	1057a.	6
WILLIAM TOWNSEND	Point Look Out	100a.	1
LUKE TOWNSEND	Powells Lott 100a. Burnt Marsh 200a.	300a.	0
GEORGE TAYLOR	Goodwill	50a.	5
JOSEPH TIMMONS	Dearfield	50a.	8
ELIJAH TIMMONS	Elijahs Purchase	50a.	9
SAMUEL TAYLOR	Winchester	313a.	3
THOMAS TIMMONS	Double Purchase 69a. Straban 48a.	117a.	5
STEPHEN TIMMONS	Enlargement	73a.	5
MARY TRUITT	Truitts Choice	119a.	4
CALEB TINGLE	Temple Hall 242a. Double Purchase 84a. Gun Shot Ridge 100a. Calebs Discovery 79½a. Hopkins Choice 50a. Conclusion 116a. Lands End 15a. Mitchells D. Park 24a. Hillards Discovery 37½a. Tingles Addition 12a. Lands End Enlarged 25a.	795a.	12
NEHEMIAH TRUITT	Belfast	90½a.	2
WILLIAM TRUITT	Belfast	90½a.	6
ISAAC TAYLOR	none		4
SARAH TIMMONS	Double Purchase	34½a.	1
WILLIAM P. TRUITT	none		5
BENJAMIN TIMMONS	none		4
BARSHEBA TAYLOR	none		3
JOHN TURNER	none		6
JOHN TAYLOR	none		7
MARY TULL	none		1
LEVIN TIMMONS	none		3
LOVINAH TUBBS	none		5
JOHN TUBBS	none		6
ARMWELL VIGEROUS	none		1
ISHMAEL WILLIAMS	Williams Inheritance 96a.	96a.	14
ESAU WILLIAMS	Williams Inheritance 96a. Partnership 50a.	146a.	10
REBECCA WILLIAMS	Williams Inheritance	7a.	2

BUCKINGHAM 100

OWNERS NAME	LAND	TOTAL ACRES	White Inhab.
NATHANIEL WILLIAMS	Williams Inheritance	40a.	8
JOHN DRAGOO	none		6
ISAAC DUNCAN	Golden Quarter	212a.	0
ISAAC DUNCAN	Golden Quarter	212a.	0
JOHN DAGSWORTHY	Wilderness	600a.	0
WILLIAM EVANS Sr.	none		5
WILLIAM EVANS Jr.	none		1
JOSEPH EVANS	Green Swamp 104a. Williams Lott 36a. Desart 80a. Bear Quarter 98a. Luck In Time 15a.	333a.	8
ZENO EVANS	Endeavor	72a.	5
GAMAGE EVANS	none		7
JOHN EVANS	none		5
ISAAC EVANS	Friendship 59a. Mt.Pleasand 117a. ____?Advice 24a.	200a.	9
SARAH EVANS	none		3
ELIZABETH EVANS	Long Acre & Friendship	70a.	5
PEAL FRANKLIN	Franklins Security	60a.	7
WILLIAM FASSIT	Carmell 300a. Meadow 100a. Buckingham 441a. Freemans Lot 96a.	937a.	4
JOHN FRANKLIN Sr.	Franklins Security	250a.	12
JOHN FASSITT Sr.	Goshen & Mayfields 232a. Turvills Advenute 370a. Joseph's Venture 50a.	652a.	9
ROUSE FASSITT	Holly Swamp 5a. Goshen & Mayfields 460a.	465a.	3
JAMES FASSITT	Chestnut Level 46a. Morehusk 228a. Archibalds Discovery 50a. Fishing Harbour 25a.	349a.	7
WILLIAM FRANKLIN of Edwd.	Choice 88a. Security	199a.	5
SAMUEL FRANKLIN	Beachsolvania	40a.	0
JOHN FASSITT Jr.	Goshen & Mayfield 376a. Fishing Harbour 24a. Don't Puzzle 330a.	730a.	2
HENRY FRANKLIN	Partnership 100a. Franklins Adventure 20a. Burley 100a. Creedwell 22a.	242a.	6
WILLIAM FRANKLIN of Wm.	Creedwell 24a. Venture	84a.	5
JOHN FRANKLIN of Wm.	Creedwell	64a.	8
JOHN FARWELL	Farwells Conclusion 34a. Farwells Folly 16a.	50a.	7
DAVID WILLIAMS	Williams Inheritance 49a. Northfield 13a. Partnership 50a.	122a.	6
THOMAS WATTS	NewPort Pannell 252a. Bowins Discovery 10a.	262a.	8
OBED WATTS	Newport Pannell	33 1/3a.	3
JOHN WATTS	none		5
DAVID WEBB	none		2
RIZDON WILLIAMS	Williams Discovery	75a.	7
SETH WHALEY	Luck in Time	51a.	3
CHARLES WHALE	Hog Quarter	50a.	4
CHARLES WHALE Jr.	none		3
CALEB WYATT	Grays Lott 33½a. Hardship 30a. Friendship 67a. R____?Venture	138½a.	7

BUCKINGHAM 100

OWNERS NAME	LAND	TOTAL ACRES	White Inhab.
WILLIAM WHITE	Buckingham	459a.	4
SARAH WARREN	Racliffs Discovery	25a.	4
JAMES WARREN	Rackliffs Discovery	80a.	3
JOSEPH WHITE	none		3
THOMAS WILDGOOSE	Windsor Forrest	80a.	1
THOMAS WELDON	none		3
JOHN WILKERSON	none		6
THOMAS WARRINGTON	C____? Hill	100a.	7.
WILLIAM WEBB	none		10
WILLIAM WEBB	none		10
JOSEPH WATSON	none		2
WILLIAM WATSON	none		2
JOHN WATSON	none		3
SARAH WYATT	none		2
JOHN WHITE	Buckingham	75a.	8
THOMAS WHORTON	none		3
MARTHA WATERS	none		3
JOSEPH WATERS	Security 34a. Friends Good will 33a. Northampton 100a. Southampton 230a.	397a.	10
SARAH? WARREN	Rackliffs Discovery165a.	165a.	6
John? WARREN of Wm.	Rackliffs Discovery	50a.	1
____ WARREN	Dennis's Discovery	758a.	5
PHILLIP WHITE	Fishing Harbour 395a. Endeavour 200a. Unknown 150a.	745a.	4
ROBERT YOUNG	Chance	150a.	0
ISAAC AYRES	none		6
JACOB ADAMS for Gertrude Adams, Wilderness Addition to Desert		200a.	0
JOHN BRADFORD	Golden Neck	50a.	6
ROBERT MITCHELL	Conclusion 40a. Peters Chance 50a.	90a.	1
WILLIAM MELSON	Hickmans Venture 23a. Retirement 27a. Good Intent 50a.	100a.	2
ELIAS MASON	none		7
WILLIAM MERRILL	Newport Lott	100a.	6
SAMUEL MILLS	none		2
JAMES MUMFORD	none		2
JESSEE MUMFORT	Vernon Dean	300a.	3
JOSHUA MASSEY	none		0
PHILLIP MARSH	none		0
JOHN MARSHALL	Mill Angle 260a. Tanton 150a. Scanderoon 75a.	485a.	0
WILLIAM Maul?	Kilkenny	200a.	4
BENJAMIN McCORMICK	Venture	67a.	0
WILLIAM MORRIS Esq.	Unity 650a. Partnership	750a.	0
ROBERT McCRAY'sheirs	Pasture Lott 40a.		0
ISABELLE MILLER	Enlargement	110a.	2
JEMIMA MORRIS	none		0
SARAH MORRIS	none		3
REBECCA MUMFORD	none		2
SMART NEWBOLD Jr.	Security	85a.	4
POWELL PENNEWELL	none		8
ZADOCK PURNELL Jr.	none		2
JOHN POSTLEY	Powells Purchase 9a. Richardsons Ridge 8a. Wheel of Fortune 338a. Beacholfania 48a.	395a.	6

BUCKINGHAM 100

OWNERS NAME	LAND	TOTAL ACRES	WHITE INHAB.
THOMAS POWELL Jr.	Powells Security 130a.	130a.	6
ZADOCK POWELL	Zadocks Security, Poor Choice 215a.		11
MORDICA POWELL	none		7
THOMAS PURNELL	Genezar 432a. Goshen & Mayfield 152a. Winchester 362a. Atkinsons heirs 200a. Worcester 50a. Timber Grove 1283a. Rackliffs Lott 33a. Purnells Venture 60a. Mumfords Lott 22a. My Fortune 78a. Harrisons Lott 80a. Hollands Endeavour 130a. Holly Grove 80a.	2860a.	4
THOMAS PURNELL-ditto-for Atkinsons Heirs		200a.	0
SOLOMON PURKINS	Tanton 100a. Emmits Discovery 33a.	133a.	3
THOMAS POWELL Sr.	Powells Security	150a.	2
THOMAS PURKINS	Inch & Troublesome	173a.	6
JOHN POWELL	none		2
ZADOCK PURNELL	Genezar 432a. Pleasant 432a. Orkney 80a. Discovery 100a.	1046a.	4
WALTON PURNELL	Security 702a. Addition to Holy Grove 432a. Hog Quarter 374a. ½ of Grist Mill 50a.	1556a.	9
ELIJAH PURNELL	none		3
ZENETH POWELL, widow	WildCat Den 130a.	130a.	7
LEVI PEPPER	none		4
PETER PARKER Jr.	Neighborhood	180a.	0
HILLARY PITT	Powells PIrchase	200a.	7
BELITHA POWELL	Richardsons Ridge	141a.	2
LEVI POWELL	none		6
THOMAS PRIDEAUX	Brotherhood 336a. Whealors Adventure 400a. Prideaux Discovery 5a. Conclusion 20a. Content 16a. TImmons Hard Luck 50a. Beachfylvania 36a. Racoon Ridge 60a. Fox Harbour 49a. Addn. to Prideaux Discovery 54a. Long Acre 24a. Goshan 225a. Lott 75a.	1683a.	3
H.E. PURNELL	Hoshen	275a.	6
PATEY POWELL	Patys Chance 143a. Pleasant Garden 100a. Silver & Penny Street 163a. Addn. to Holy Grove 98a.	504a.	9
THOMAS PURNELL Jr.	none		3
MARY PURNELL	none		0
BENJAMIN QUILLAN	Winchester 100a.	100a.	5
SAMUEL QUILLAN	none		5
ELIZABETH QUILLAN	none		1
JOHN QUILLAN	none		4
ELISHA QUILLAN	none		6
CLEMENT QUILLAN	none		6
JOHN RACKLIFFE	Genezar 500a. Goshen & May fields 170a. Pleasant 120a. Rackliffs Good Luck 200a. Beyond Expecation 274a. Newport Pannel 300a. Spanish Oak Ridge 50a. Canagogig 50a. Swamp 170a. Josepha Folly 50a.	1884a.	4

BUCKINGHAM 100

OWNERS NAME	LAND	TOTAL ACRES	White Inhab.
JOHN RANKIN	land 200a. Lott In NewPort	200a.	3
ANN RYLY	Newport Pannell 150a. Bowins Disocvery 67a.	217a.	6
NEHEMIAH KNOX	Carmell	138a.	3
JOHN KIRBY	Dixon Hill	152a.	1
JAMES KING	Hamblings Folly 65a. Lukes Hill 100a.	165a.	3
WILLIAM KENNETT	Crooked Lane	7 3/4a.	7
MARTHA LEWIS	No. Fleet	56a.	8
JOHN LENDALL	Endeavor 150a. Peters Choice 164a.	214a.	8
THOMAS LAMBERSON	Batchelors Lott 54a. Hill Glass 2 3/4a.	56 3/4a.	5
SAMUEL LOCKWOOD	Hardship	10a.	6
LEVIN LEWIS	none		4
ELISHA LAWRENCE	Cropton	113a.	5
NICHOLAS LEWIS	none		5
JACOB LYNCH	none		5
JOHN LYNCH	none		5
SMITH LINGO	HogQuarter 50a. Luck in time 4a.	54a.	8
MARY LAWRENCE	Cropton 66 2/3a.	66 2/3a.	2
NEHEMIAH LATCHUM	Newington Green, Smiths Choice Holland Disocvery	268a.	3
Jo^a. K. LATCHUM	Hollands Discovery, Smiths Choice	100a.	4
DAVID LYNCH	Friends Assistance	100a.	4
JAMES LEWIS	Windsor Forrest 184a. Josephs Addition 55a. Conveniency	258a.	7
SOLOMON LONG	unknown	164a.	0
ELIZABETH LONG	Security	116a.	0
LEVIN MILLS	Bowins Discovery 90½a.	90½a.	5
DUNCAN MURRAY	Diour 257a. Pasture Lott 94a. Burtons Chance 86a.	217a.	4
CHARITY MASSEY	Carmel	160a.	2
JOHN MASSEY	Carmel 110a. Buck Ridge 203a. Pleasant Lott 46a. Egds Choice 25a.	384a.	7
SARAH MASSEY	Silver & Penny Street 41a. Pleasant Lott 35a.	71a.	3
JOSIAH MITCHELL	Straban 322a. Hopkins Chance 160a. Dear Park 390a. Friendship 72a.	844a.	9
THOMAS McNEILE	Pleasant Hill	75a.	5
JAMES MUMFORD Jr.	none		2
JOHN MILLER	Troy Town 169a. Partners Content 500a.	669a.	9
GOERGE MAGEE	none		6
JOSHUA MITCHELL	Port Royall 10a. Little Purchase 30a. Conclusion 356½a.	396½a.	2
WILLIAM HICKMAN	none		2
JOSHUA HICKMAN	none		5
SETH HUDSON	none		3

BUCKINGHAM 100

OWNERS NAME	LAND	TOTAL ACRES	White Inhab.
___ HUDSON	Harrygate 250a. Hardship 144a. Addn. to head of Middle Branch 133a.	523a.	1
SARAH HENRY	Goshen & May fields	350a.	1
HENRY HUDSON	Patys Discovery	366a.	9
DENNIS HUDSON	none		9
Saml ? HUDSON Jr.	Powells Lott	39a.	2
JOB HUDSON	Powells Lott	39a.	5
ELIHU HAZZARD	none		5
DAVID HUDSON	none		5
SAMUEL JOHNSON	Three Brothers 190a. Cornhill 75a.	265a.	6
LABIN JOHNSON	Supply 148a. Oak Hall 367a. Beach Point 95a. Beach Ridge 53a. Hair Point 50a. Beachshylvania 70a.	780a.	1
DAVID JOHNSON	Three Brothers	181a.	0
ROBERT JOHNSON	Three Brothers	214a.	7
HANNAH JOHNSON	Three Brothers	90 3/4a.	1
ELEANOR JONES	none		2
WILLIAM IRONSHIRE	Tribble Purchase 517a. Friends Advice 24a. Last Choice & Adventure 15½a. Small Purchase 3 3/4a. Bellfast 169a. Coventons Choice 221½a. Timber Grove 193a. Small Lott 10a. Jobs Fishing Hole 50a. Ironshires Discovery 45a. Straban & Addn. 347a. Davisons Beginning 365a. White Oak Swamp 206a. Gift to my 1st. Son 6a.	2062a.	3
JOHN JONES Sr.	St.Martins Desert	152a.	0
WILLIAM JONES	Oak Hall	115a.	5
JOSEPH JONES	Oak Hall	60a.	10a.
JOHN JARMAN	none		3
THOMAS JONES Sr.	none		7
STEPHEN JUSTICE	Desert 200a. Stepehnsons Island 49a.	249a.	9
ESTHER IRONSHIRE	none		3
SUSANNAH KENNETT	Gift 150a. Cornhills Addn.	180a.	6
KENDAL KENNETT	Conclusion 23a. Eagle Point	123a.	4
ELIZABETH KENNETT	Eagle Point	50a.	1
JOHN HOWARD Jr.	none		5
WILLIAM HOWARD	none		5
Dr.John Howard Sr.	Hog Quarter	100a.	8
BENJAMIN HAMBLIN	Wilderness 34½a. Hamblins Lott 35½a.	70a.	3
WILLIAM HILL	Mt.Pleasant	112½a.	7
HAMPTON HOPKINS	Eagle Point 464a.	6	
COMFORT HENDERSON	none		6
EDWARD HENRY	Addn. to Fair Meadow Rectified 535a.		1
WARREN HADDER	Northfleet	200a.	8
WILLIAM HENDERSON	none		4
ELIZABETH HADDER	Gilleland	100a.	2
JOHN HADDER	none		7
WILLIAM HOZIER	none		6

BUCKINGHAM 100

OWNERS NAME	LAND	TOTAL ACRES	White Inhab.
JESSE HOLLOWAY	land	114a.	9
RACHEL HUDSON	Venture Security, Endeavour 255a.	255a.	6
JAMES HALL	Creedwell	65a.	2
RICHARD AHLL	Neighborhood	183a.	9
ELIJAH HOLLOWAY	Cropton	60a.	6
THOMAS HOLLOWAY	Addition to Now 133a. Teagues Content 100a. NOW ADDN. 100a, and 75a.	408a.	8
EBENEZER HOLLOWAY	none		3
JAMES HOLLOWAY	none		2
SOLOMON HOLLOWAY	none		5
MOSES HOLLOWAY Jr.	none		8
AARON HOLLOWAY Jr.	none		3
LEVI HOLLOWAY	Tilberry Swamp	75a.	4
MOSES & AARON HOLLOWAY	Moses Lott 100a. New Addn. to Old 132a. Late at Night 50a. Now Addn. 63½a. Labour in Vain 339 3/4a. Dales Discovery 100a.	786¼a.	10
McKIMMY HUDSON	Genezar 200a. Whalleys Discovery 15a.	215a.	6
JOSEPH HAMBLIN	Golden Pleasure	100a.	3
TABITHA HUDSON	Powells Lott	39a.	1
TAMPLIN HANCOCK	none		3
F.I. HENRY	Buckland 1793a. Jesemain 102a. Bald Eagel 32a. Second Choice 81a.	2006a.	0
ISAAC HILL	Mt. Pleasant	99a.	1
JOSIAH HOPKINS	none		7
LABIN HILL	Gilliland	100a.	8
ANN HUDSON	Harry Gate 250a. Hardship 340a. Grist Mill 50a. Hudsons Delay 20a. Powells Lott ?	660+a.	1
JOHN BAKER	none		4
HENRY BELL	Robins Discovery 130a. Desart 171½a. unknown 200a. Carrys Chance 50a. Wilderness Addn. to Desart 30a. Polks Neglect 295a Cratons Lott 75a. Chance 60a. Forrest Flower 60a. Bear Quarter 47a.	1118a.	12
ANN BRATTEN	Cropton & Morrisville?, Addn. to Crooked Lott	270a.	4
WHITTINGTON BOWIN Jr.	Timber Grove & Truitts Choice	230a.	1
ISAAC BRADFORD	Martins Desert	40a.	6
WILLIAM BAYNUM	Baynums Purchase	100a.	9
WILLIAM BRATTEN Sr.	Beachsylvania 120a. Buck Ridge 244a.	364a.	4
ADAM BRATTAN	HogPen 18a. Cumberland 40a.	58a.	3
ISAAC BRATTEN	Cumberland	20a.	1
WILLIAM BRATTEN Jr.	Cumberland	20a.	1
JOHN BENSON	none		8
GILBERT BEEDLE	none		3

BUCKINGHAM 100

OWNERS NAME	LAND	TOTAL ACRES	WHITE INHAB.
SAMUEL BRATTEN	Mt.Pleasant 100a. Turkey Point 50a. Luck in Time 50a.	200a.	8
WILLIAM BOWEN	Goshen	272a.	3
ROBERT BELL	none		0
LEVIN BRADFORD	none		9
ESTHER BALLARD	none		6
WHITTINGTON BOWEN Sr.	none		6
DANIEL COX BETHARD	none		4
BENJAMIN BETHARD	none		2
LEVIN BAKER	none		9
JOHN COX	Cox's Addition	110a.	6
ISA COX	Cox's Addition	82a.	1
LYDA COX	Cox's Addition	41a.	5
MARY COLLINS	Miserable Quarter	150a.	6
JAMES CONNER	HogsNorton 27a. Turners Hall 40a.	67a.	5
LEVIN COFFIN	Nortons Desire	100a.	8
AVERY COX	Cox's Addition	106a.	6
JOHN C. CROPPER	Smiths Choice, Hollands Discovery Newington Green	375a.	8
AVERY CORDRAY	Cropton	80a.	3
BELITHA COLLINS	Temple Hall, Showells Addn. Croptons & Littleworth	114a.	6
JOHN CURRIN	Maidens Blush	9a.	6
REUBEN CROPPER	Reubins Addition	9a.	1
NATHANIEL CROPPER Jr.	none		8
JESSE CROPPER Sr.	Croppers Discovery	100a.	7
JAMES RACKLIFFE	unreadable		
NATHANIEL RACKLIFFE	unreadable	64?a.	2
SARAH RAMSEY	unknown	100a.	2
CHARLES RATCLIFFE	Tanton 130a. Scanderoon 70a.	200a.	5
JOHN RION	Addn.to Whealors Adv.	100a.	3
WILLIAM ROBINS	Genezar 80a. Robins Discovery	89a.	0
ISABELLE ROBINS	none		4
HILL ROUND	Landing in Synepuxent	367a.	5
THOMAS ROLAND	none		2
WILLIAM ROAN	Verdon Dean 50a. Showells Discovery 150a.	200a.	1
MATT ROAN	Showells Disocvery	100a.	1
CHARLES RATCLIFFE Jr.	Dont Puzzle 320a. Hilliards Discovery 200a. Goshan 100a.	620a.	0
LITTLETON ROBINS	W___?'s Heirs	100a.	0
NATHANIEL RICHARDS	Happy Entrance	170a.	2
LEVIN RYLEY	Creedwell	29a.	5
SARAH ROAN	none		4
JOHN STEWART	Showells Addnition	150a.	13
THOMAS SELBY	Addn. to Whartons Adventure 200a. Poplar Neck 54 3/4a. Freemans Lott 96a. Kilkeny 27a.	377 3/4a.	0
JOHN SCHOOLFIELD	Collins Security	166a.	5
GEORGE STEVENSON	Goshen	147a.	4
JOHN SEARS	Dion	8a.	2
THOMAS SMITH	Smiths Industry	113a.	7
MARY SMOCK	none		2
LEVI SMITH	Smiths Industry	50a.	5
HENRY SCHOOLFIELD	none		4

BUCKINGHAM 100

OWNERS NAME	LAND	TOTAL ACRES	White Inhab.
JOHN SMITH	Smiths Chance	86a.	10a.
JOHN O. N. SMITH	Happy Entrance, Whites Addition	250a.	3
JOHN SHOWELL	Cropton	40a.	3
JOHN STEVENS	Endeavor 70a. Addition 69a. Stevens Chance 15a.	154a.	4
JOSHUA STEVENS	land	75a.	0
RACHEL STEWART	none		2
STEPHEN SMOCK	none		0
DANIEL SELBY	Windsor Forrest	80a.	5
HENRY SNEAD	Troublesome	13a.	4
WILLIAM STEVENSON	Mt.Pleasant 104a. Mitchells D.Park 225a. Pinders Neglect 12a. Buckingham 52a.	393s.	4

William Richardson   MATTAPONY 100   MALES-FEMALES
    assessor

			MALES-FEMALES
HENRY AYRES	Watts Conviency	704a.	5 - 2
LEAH AYRES	NONE		4 - 1
BENJAMIN AYDELOTTE	Falmouth 200a. Peterson 160a. MIFFLINS DISCOVERY 36a. Black Ridge 243a.	639a.	3 - 3
BENJAMIN AYDELOTTE	of Wm. Little & Drakes House 120a.	120a.	1 - 2
JOSHUA ALLEN	Parramores Double Purchase 40a. Willitts Outlett 15½a.	65½a.	2 - 4
JAMES AYDELOTTE	Batchellors Lott	129a.	1 - 3
JOHNALLEN Sr.	Allens Industry	207a.	2 - 1
ZADOCK ARDIS	(Fisher Walthum Security)		0 - 0
ISHMAEL ANDREWS	none		1 - 2
STEPHEN ALLEN	Ceadar Grove,Venture Prevention	611a.	3 - 5
WILLIAM AGNAFIELD	Willins Discovery	50a.	1 - 2
JOHN ALLEN Jr.	(John Allen Security)		0 - 0
MARY ALLEN	none		0 - 2
JOHN ALLEN	Parramores Double Purchase 40a. Willitts Outlett 15¼a.	55½a.	2 - 1
JOHN BELL	Junoteague	140a.	2 - 1
LEVIN BELL	none		2 - 2
ALEXANDER McKallen	none		0 - 0
GEORGE BAKER	none		2 - 4
WILLIAM BRASURE	none		3 - 4
BENJAMIN BONNAWILL	Wakefieldd 200a. Wakefields Discovery 200a.	400a.	6 - 3
EZEKIEL BRUMBLE	Rotten Quarter Addition 15a. Pine Hopes 325a.	340a.	3 - 4
JAMES BLAKE	(John Ridding Security)none		0 - 0
ELIZABETH BRITTINGHAM	Timber Quarter	50a.	1 - 5
JOHN BRITTINGHAM	New Timber Quarter	60a.	2 - 2
THOMAS BRITTINGHAM	none		4 - 1
OLIVER BLAKE	(michael Tarr Security)		0 - 0
AARON BLAKE	(Wm.Selby of Capt.John.Security)		0 - 0
ELISHA BRITTINGHAM	none		2 - 5

William Richardson assessor of MATTAPONY 100

OWNERS NAME	LAND	TOTAL Acres	White Inhab. MALE-FEMALE
LEVI BEACHBOARD	Purgatory 44a. Claywells Security 56a. Newark 40a. Come by Chance 33a.	173a.	3 - 1
CHARLES BENNETT	none		0 - 0
BENJAMIN PURNELL	Hills? Chance	5a.	1 - 1
JABEZ PILCHARD	Little Harbour	36a.	3 - 3
ESAU PILCHARD	Smithfield	50a.	3 - 3
Capt.JOHN PETTIGNU	Moscito Point	440a.	1 - 5
ELIJAH PILCHARD	Long Point	120a.	3 - 3
SOLOMON PEPPER	Mulberry Heath	200a.	2 - 6
ROBERT P. YELVERTON	Conviency	154a.	3 - 3
Capt.JOHN PARREMOUR	Parremours Double Purchase	900a.	4 - 3
Major PHILLIP QUINTON	BlackRidge	50a.	0 - 0
RICHARD ROWLEY	Peterson 90a. Falmouth 100a.	190a.	4 - 4
BOWDEN ROBINS	Robins Partnership 109a. Jinoteague 76a. Friendship 90a.	475a.	1 - 2
DANIEL ROBINS	Jinateague	200a.	2 - 2
JOSHUA RIGGIN	Tannors Hall	150a.	3 - 3
JOHN ROBINSON	Robinsons Partnership	73a.	2 - 2
JOSIAH ROBINSON	Robinsons Partnership	73a.	1 - 0
LEVI ROBINSON	Robinsons Partnership	73a.	1 - 0
JOHN RODNEY	Mulberry Heath 50a. Tobias Disappointment 100a.	150a.	4 - 4
LEVIN REID	CartWheel	100a.	3 - 4
MARY REID	Eanton?	80a.	5 - 4
GEORGE RICHARDSON	none		0 - 0
ROBERT RICHARDSON	Willshire	150a.	2 - 3
WILLIAM RICHARDSON	Conclusion 23a. Wilshire 350a. Lamb? Hammock 132a.	505a.	5 - 3
JOHN SCARBROUGH	none		0 - 0
HUGH STEVENSON	Conviency 120a. Castle Hill 92a.	212a.	3 - 2
SAMUEL SCARBROUGH	Timber Quarter	300a.	0 - 0
OUTTEN STURGIS	Pharsallia 250a. King Harrys Neck 292a.	542a.	2 - 5
DANIEL STEVENS	Pharsalia	50a.	0 - 0
GEORGE STEWART	King Harrys Neck	181a.	0 - 0
Capt.JOHN SELBY	Bantry 1050a. Brothers Love 150a. Piney Island 126a. Bastable 4a. Good Hope 62a. Cold Harbour 45a. Bermuda 20a.	1357a.	3 - 3
JAMES SELBY of John,	Tinderdale 135a. Forlorn & Mills 9a. Wild Cat 40a. Chance 50a. Friendship 100a.	334a.	1 - 1
JOHN SELBY of Parker,	Timber Quarter, Key 36a.	286a.	2 - 1
PARKER SELBY	Middlemore	26 3/4a.	0 - 0
COMFORT MERRILL	Claywells Security 33½a. Yarmouth 20a.	53½a.	1 - 3
SARAH MERRILL	ditto & Ditto	166 3/4a.	0 - 2
JOHN MILBORN	Hedley Hill 300a. Rome 74a. Milbourns Meadow 41a.	415a.	4 - 3

WILLIAM RICHARDSON, Assessor of MATTAPONY 100

OWNERS NAME	LAND	TOTAL ACRES	White Inhab. MALE-FEMALE
JOSEPH MERRILL	King Harrys Neck	79a.	2 - 1
URIAH McHENRY	none		1 - 2
ELIZABETH McHENRY	none		1 - 2
SMITH MELVIN	Hog Quarter 70a. Partnership 50a.	120a.	3 - 3
JONATHAN MELVIN	none		1 - 3
THOMAS MADDUX	Barren Quarter	200a.	0 - 0
THOMAS MARTIN	none		0 - 0
DANIEL MIFFLIN	Asateague 100a. Bermuda 74a. Jinoteague 15a. Mifflins Discovery 56½a. Pharsalla 713a. Thornbury 100a. Mifflins Pasturage 40a.	1098a.	0 - 0
WILLIAM NEWTON	Hogs Choice	211a.	3 - 3
SELBY NEWTON	Poor Choice, Bastable	150a.	0 - 0
MARY NELSON	Brothers Help	75a.	3 - 5
MOSES NELSON	Conveniency 150a. surplus land 25a.	175a.	5 - 4
JONATHAN NELSON	none		2 - 3
JESSE NELSON	Hardship Branch	160a.	0 - 0
HUGH NELSON	Hammer 213a. for Mrs.Williams	213a.	1 - 1
LEVIN NEWTON	Parramors Double Purchase	100a.	2 - 4
ABRAHAM NEWTON	none		2 - 3
JOHN PURNELL	Pharsalia 142a. Purnells Orchard 206a.	348a.	1 - 2
JOHN PURNELL of John,	Mattapony Marsh 240a. Purnells Lott 167a. Brothers Love 357a.	764a.	1 - 0
JOHN PRICE	none		4 - 2
JOHN PATRICK	none		2 - 2
WILLIAM PRICE	Bridgewater	212a.	4 - 5
JOHN PRICE Jr.	(Severon Johnson Security)		1 - 0
WILLIAM PRUITT	Pruitts Choice 50a. Bridgewater 46a.	96a.	3 - 3
SACKER PARKER	Wakefield	100a.	0 - 0
ELIZABETH PAYNE	Smithfield	72a.	1 - 2
LEVIN PAYNE	Smithfield	72½a.	2 - 2
ISAAC HENDERSON	Turtle Ridge 70a. Tinderdale	146a.	3 - 1
WILLIAM HOUSTON	none		1 - 4
WILLIAM HARRISON	none		2 - 4
BRITTINGHAM HENDERSON	Littleworth	100a.	2 - 2
LEVIN HILL	Robinsosn Inheritance	470a.	4 - 4
WILLIAM HANDCOCK	Lanes Choice 100a. Handcocks Choice 20a.	120a.	4 - 5
JOHN JOHNSON	Chance	45a.	1 - 1
GILES JONES	Peppers Vexation	5a.	1 - 2
JONATHAN HEUTT	(Levin Bell Security)		0 - 0
SAMUEL JOHNSON	Carrigonstick 150a. Ditto & timber 54a. Arrsashen 70a.	274a.	3 - 3
LEVINIA JOHNSON	none		0 - 1
DANIEL JOHNSON	none		3 - 5
SEVERON Johnson	for Mitchells relations	103a.	2 - 4
DIANNIA JOHNSON	for Mitchells relations	95a.	1 - 3
ELIAKIM JOHNSON	Bridgewater 102a. Addn. to Thornberry 112a.Cypress Point 45a.	259a.	3 - 8

William Richardson, assessor of MATTAPONY 100

OWNERS NAME	LAND	TOTAL ACRES	White Inhab. MALE-FEMALE
HEZEKIAH JOHNSON	Batchelors Lott 112a. Bridgewater 130a.	142a.	2 - 3
JOHN JOHNSON	Purgatory 204a. Puzzle 10a. pt.Purgatory 50a.	264a.	2 - 3
JAMES JOHNSON	Purgatory	70a.	1 - 1
ANN JONES	Addn. to Allens Survey	190a.	0 - 3
ELISHA JONES	Thornberry	65½a.	1 - 1
JOHN JONES Jr.	Pagans, Batchelors Adventure 100a. Jones Addn. to Giles Addition 73a.	173a.	5 - 3
JOHN JONES Sr.	Dublin, Assateague 66a.	366a.	5 - 2
LEAH JONES	none		0 - 0
WILLIAM KELLAM	Smithfield	175a.	3 - 6
JOHN KELLAM	Yarmouth 225a. Claywell Security 229a. Key 7a.	461a.	3 - 7
JOHN LAMBERSON	Robins Partnership	109a.	1 - 2
ELIZABETH LAMBDON	none		1 - 2
RACHELL LAMBERSON	Robinsons Partnership	50a.	1 - 3
JAMES LINZEY Sr.	Mill Branch 200a. Linzeys Purchase 75a. Luck 10a.	285a.	1 - 1
JAMES LINZEY Jr.	none		3 - 2
GOERGE LAYFIELD	Lott 50a. Funn 100a.	150a.	3 - 5
JAMES MARTIN	(Virginia Line		3 - 1
PARKER DUKES	unknown	116a.	2 - 3
WILLIAM DUKES	none		2 - 1
ELIZABETH DUKES	none		1 - 4
JESSE DICKERSON	Temple Comb 100a. Chance & Lock 60a. Davis Discovery 70a.	230a.	3 - 3
REBECCA DAVIS	Timber Quarter 36a. Davis's Security 79a.	115a.	3 - 3
ALEXANDER DAVIS	Old Berry	100a.	1 - 3
NATHANIEL DAVIS	Purgatory 131a. Davis's Security 90a. Assateague Beach 50a.	271a.	2 - 2
JOHN FLOYD	none		1 - 2
AYRES GREER	Littleworth	165a.	2 - 3
MAJOR GAGE	Jincoteague	100a.	0 - 0
JAMES GUTHRY	(Joshua Guthry Security)		1 - 0
DAVID GIVONS	none		4 - 4
NELLY GUTHRY	none		2 - 1
JOSHUA GUTHRY	Conviency 60a. White Oak Swamp 16a.	76a.	4 - 3
ROBERT GIBBS	none		5 - 3
SAMUEL HUDSON	Now Enlarged	200a.	7 - 5
NEHEMIAH HOLLAND	Selbys Neglect 51a. Friendship 67a. Purnells Adventure 50a. Translvinia 100a. Timber Quarter 150a. Fox Harbour 96a. Allens Industry 22a. Chance 50a. Bastable 14a.	690a.	6 - 4
LEVIN HOPKINS	Nunsgreen 277a. Middlemore 25a. Poplar Hill 27a.	326a.	4 - 5
LEVIN HILL-shoemaker	(Levin Hopkins Security)		1 - 0
SAMUEL HOPKINS	Purgatory 55a. Come by Chance 79a.		3 - 3

William Richardson, assessor of MATTAPONY 100

OWNERS NAME	LAND	TOTAL ACRES	White Inhab. MALE-FEMALE
JOHN HANDCOCK	Jinoteague	100a.	4 - 5
WILLIAM KELLAM	Purnells Lott	473a.	3 - 4
WILLIAM HILL	Middleton 200a. Halls Addition 50a. Poplar Hill 97a.	347a.	3 - 5
Capt. JOHN HILL	Nunsgreen	13a.	1 - 3
JOHNSON HILL	none		2 - 3
WILSON HAMMOND	Weavours Choice 70a. Key 22a.	92a.	2 - 3
MOSES HUDSON	(Labin Hudson Security)		1 - 0
MATTHEW HOPKINS	none		6 - 2
BENJAMIN HOLLAND	Johnsons Hope	300a.	1 - 4
EPHRAIM HENDERSON	Parramour Double Purchase	207a.	3 - 3
WILLIAM HENDERSON	Fludberry & Mill	160a.	1 - 2
LABIN HUDSON	Selbys Double Purchase 117a. Parramours Double Purchase 25a. Oldbud Survey 100a.	242a.	2 - 4
ELI TARR Jr.	none		1 - 1
JOHN TUNNELL	none		4 - 4
JOHN TOWNSEND	none		2 - 5
MICHAEL TARR Jr.	New Timber Quarter	100a.	3 - 4
BENJAMIN TULL	(John Allen Sr. Security)		1 - 0
JOHN TULL	young man		1 - 0
ELIJAH TARR	Allins Addition	100a.	1 - 5
DANIEL TURNER	young man		1 - 0
GEORGE TRUITT	Middleton 100a. Friends Assistance 50a.	150a.	1 - 3
JAMES TARR	(Severon Johnson Security)		1 - 0
SMITH TURNER	none		3 - 1
MICHAEL TARR of Samuel,	Mitchells Mill Branch	124 3/4a.	1 - 0
JOSHUA TARR	(Michael Tarr of Samuel Security)		1 - 0
OBED TAYLOR	Willitts Discovery	50a.	1 - 0
JOHN TARR Jr.	Middlemore	107a.	2 - 2
STATON TRADER	Pilchards Neglect	100a.	3 - 1
JOHN TAYLOR	Bacon Quarter 100a. Reids Contrivance 100a. Conviency	300a.	6 - 4
THOMAS TAYLOR	Taylors Lott, 70a. M___ Discovery 50a.	120a.	3 - 3
JOHN TINDALL	none		6 - 2
SARAH TAYLOR	Temple Comb	100a.	1 - 4
SAMUEL TARR Jr.	Pharsallia	150a.	2 - 3
MICHAEL TARR Sr.	Kilkeny 16½a. New Timber Quarter 111a.	127½a.	1 - 2
ESTHER TURNER	Thornerrry	51a.	1 - 2
WILLIAM TURNER	Thornberry	100a.	0 - 0
JOHN TARR Sr.	Shafsberry 126a. Oldfields Swamp 130a.	256a.	3 - 3
ELISHA TARR Sr.	none		1 - 4
SAMUEL TARR Sr.	Chance 42a. Tinderdale 150a.	192a.	3 - 3
RACHEL TULL	none		1 - 2
JOHN VEAZEY	Prices Discovery	125a.	2 - 2
EDWARD VANDOM	Scotts Lott 60a. Forrest of Deer 40a.	100a.	0 - 0

William Richardson, assessor of MATTAPONY 100

OWNERS NAME	LAND	TOTAL ACRES	White Inhab. MALE-FEMALE
SOUTHY VEAZEY	Venture	70a.	3 - 5
ANN VEASEY	Bermuda	92a.	0 - 2
Capt. FISHER WALTUN	Transylvania	400a.	1 - 3
SARAH WILSON	none		1 - 3
RUBIN WESTERHOUSE	none		0 - 1
WILLIAM WALTUN	Transylvania	260a.	1 - 3
JOB WALTUN	none		4 - 4
JAMES WHITE	(Benjamin Holland Security)		1 - 0
WEST WATSON	Pilchards Neglect 30a. Bacon Quarter 150a.	180a.	3 - 3
LEVIN WATSON	Forrest of Dear	63a.	3 - 2
HENRY WILLETT	none		1 - 1
JOHN WISE	unknown	300a.	0 - 0
WILLIAM SNEAD	none		0 - 0
LEAH SELBY	Castle Hill, Conviency	125a.	1 - 3
PARKER SELBY Sr.	Hogs Choice 100a. Kilkam 103½a. Tit for Tat 100a. Middlemore 25a. land of Phillip Selby 166a.	494½a.	1 - 3
PARKER SELBY of Parker,	Robinsons Inheritance	472a.	3 - 4
WILLIAM SELBY of John,	Pharsallia	350a.	1 - 2
JOHN SPENCE	Middlemore & Long Island	53½a.	0 - 0
JAMES STEVENSON	Conviency	250a.	5 - 8
RICHARD STURGIS	Widows Lott 68a. Hardship Branch 50a. Sturgis Choice 37a.	155a.	3 - 5
JOHN STURGIS of Thomas,	Chance	60a.	1 - 2
MONICA SADLER	none		2 - 2
THOMAS STURGIS	Chance	20a.	1 - 1
ROBERT SLOCUMB	Conviency	150a.	3 - 3
KENDAL SIMPSON	Friendship	100a.	4 - 4
WILLIAM SLOCOMB	(Robert Slocomb Security)		0 - 0
OUTTEN STURGIS of Thomas,	Shafsberry	67a.	1 - 3
DANIEL STURGIS, Blacksmith,	none		1 - 0
JOSHUA STURGIS	Chance, Littleworth	91a.	2 - 5
LEVIN STURGIS	Hog Quarter 100a. Timber Quarter 56s. Milbourns Savanah 23a. Goose 31a.	210a.	4 - 2
STEPHEN STURGIS	Littleworth	63a.	4 - 4
JOHN O. STURGIS	Conviency	150a.	4 - 4
SAMUEL SELBY of Micajah,	Carrgonstick	116s.	0 - 0
SARAH SELBY of Daniel,	Bastable	123a.	0 - 1
PHILLIP SELBY	Hog Quarter 150a. Cedar Grove	200a.	1 - 0
MARY SELBY of Parker-	Tobias Dissapointment & Lions Luck? & Mulberry Heath	125a.	0 - 0
RYLEY SLOCOMB	none		4 - 2
WILLIAM SELBY	Long Island	150a.	0 - 0
ALEXANDER TAYLOR	Mills Island	756a.	3 - 3
POLLY TAYLOR orphan of Elisha			0 - 1
MORGAN BRADSHER	Cypress Grove 100a. Bridge Water 30a.	130a.	2 - 0
WILLIAM BRITTINGHAM	none		1 - 0
ELIJAH BRITTINGHAM	none		1 - 0

WILLIAM RICHARDSON, assessor of MATTAPONY 100

OWNERS NAME	LAND	TOTAL ACRES	White Inhab. MALE-FEMALE
CHARLES BENNETT	Rome	100a.	4 - 3
WILLIAM BENNETT	Selbys Double Survey	90a.	1 - 4
MARY BROTHERER	Friends Assistance	50a.	3 - 3
WILLIAM BENNETT Sr.	Weavers Choice	96a.	2 - 1
WILLIAM BENNETT Jr.	Duglass Contrivance	50a.	1 - 2
SAMUEL BRITTINGHAM	Parramors Double Purchase	100a.	5 - 2
NATHANIEL BRITTINGHAM	(Daniel Robins Security)		1 - 0
DANIEL BURCH	(James Lindsey Jr. Security)		1 - 0
Capt. GEORGE BLAKE	(John Selby Security)		0 - 0
JOHN BALL	Scotts Mistake	10 3/4a.	0 - 00
JOHN CHAILLE	Oldbury 10a. Venture 50a.	60a.	6 - 3
JUSTUS CAREY	Hog Hill	100a.	0 - 0
CUSTUS CLOUDS	none		2 - 2
MARY COLLINS	none		0 - 3
SOLOMON CAREY Jr.	Dear Harbour 103a. Bilks Speedwell 100a. Addn. to Ditto 63a.	266a.	6 - 3
WILLIAM COWLEY	none		2 - 2
JEREMIAH CAREY	Land of Little	160a.	4 - 3
GLEN CILPIN	none		1 - 2
SAMUEL CLOG	none		1 - 0
EZEKIEL COSTON	Bridgewater Supply 23a. Costons Addn. 75a. Costons Chance 300a. Prices Addn. 160a. Ditto 71a. Fon 100a. Costons Folly 20a.	749a.	3 - 1
EZEKIEL COSTON	(Ezekiel Coston Sr. Security)		0 - 0
SMITH CAREY	Cyrpess Addn. 72a. Bilks Speedwell 23a.	95a.	3 - 4
JOHN CAREY of Smith	none		0 - 0
WILLIAM CONNER of Wm.	none		1 - 1
ELISHER CAREY	none		2 - 3
HIMMON COWLY	Littleworth	100a.	2 - 2
WILLIAM CRAFORD	Rome	100a.	3 - 4
MARY CARTER	none		1 - 1
BARTLETT CAMERON	Forrest of Dear 100a. Cales Choice 50a.	150a.	5 - 3
SOLOMON CAREY	none		1 - 1
JOSHUA DUER	Goose & Gander 88a. Goose 91a. Hog Quarter 10a.	189a.	0 - 0
DAVID DIXON	Cold Harbour, Conviency	125a.	5 - 5
ARTHUR DAVIS	Jingoteague	100a.	2 - 1
JOSEPH DAVIS Jr.	Jingoteague	100a.	7 - 2

Phillip Quinton, assessor of WICOMICO 100

OWNERS NAME	LAND	TOTAL ACRES	White Inhab. MALE-FEMALE
William Alliphant	Hypocrits Deceived	100a.	2 - 3
IGNATUS ANDERSON	Hypocrits Deceived Canada	165a.	5 - 4
MAGDALIN BAUSHAW	none		0 - 3
MATHIAS AUSTIN	Hoborns Chance 50a. Lott	150a.	2 - 2
WILLIAM BEAUCHAMP	none		1 - 3
LEVE BROWN	Garden Spot	50a.	2 - 3
MATHIAS AUSTIN	Austins (see above)	25a.	

PHILLIP QUINTON, Assessor of WICOMICO 100

OWNERS NAME	LAND	TOTAL ACRES	White Inhab. MALE-FEMALE
SMITH BREWINGTON	Addn. to Garden Spot 280a. Chestnut Ridge 70a.	350a.	3 - 4
JOHN BREWINGTON of Smith	(Smith Brewington Security)		1 - 0
SAMUEL BREWINGTON of Smith	(Smith Brewington Sec.)		1 - 0
ROBERT BANKS	unknown	280a.	0 - 0
WILLIAM BREWINGTON	Good Increase 123a. Wilton	209a.	2 - 2
JOHN BREWINGTON	Wilton	157a.	4 - 2
JAMES BREWINGTON	Elderbury & Wilton	130a.	3 - 3
WILLIAM BEAGLAND	(Richard Beagland Security)		1 - 0
RICHARD BEAGLAND	Smiths Discovery 76a.		3 - 3
JOHN BEAGLOW	(Richard Beaglow Sec.)		0 - 0
ELEANOR BLUITT	none		0 - 2
FREDERICK BARNCASTLE	none		2 - 2
JOHN BROWN of Jas.	Choice	75a.	3 - 4
GEORGE BROWN Sr.	Haths Chance	50a.	3 - 2
SILUS BALAY	(Setephen Dikes Security)		0 - 0
GOERGE BROWN Jr.	Haths Chance 50a. Haths Choice 50a. Browns Choice 150a.	250a.	2 - 2
HENRY BANKS	Tulls Knavery 95a. Haselton 211a.(lives in Somerset Co.)	310a.	0 - 0
JOHN CALDWELL	Smiths Discovery	100a.	1 - 1
LEVIN CAREY	Williams Chance 100a. Levins Choice 50a.	150a.	2 - 4
EZEKIEL RUARK	none		1 - 2
JONATHAN RIGGIN	Purchase 100a. Safeguard 91½a.	191¼a.	6 - 1
WILLIAM RIGGIN	none		2 - 2
JOSEPH RIGGIN	none		1 - 2
JOHN RICHARDSON	Richardsons Lott 75a. Security 31a. Piney Neck 261a.	367a.	1 - 5
BENJAMIN RYLEY	Mill Dam	80a.	0 - 0
BETTY ROBINSON	Shockleys Conclusion	60a.	1 - 2
BOWDIN ROBINS	Turkey Trap 150a. Beach Bounds 100a.	250a.	0 - 0
SOLOMON SHOCKLEY	Venture	50a.	0 - 0
GEORGE SMITH	Bacon Quarter	100a.	4 - 2
BENJAMIN SMITH	Bacon Quarter	100a.	2 - 3
LEVIN SMITH	Bacon Quarter	150a.	1 - 2
JONATHAN SHOCKLEY	Friends Good will	75a.	1 - 2
BETTY SMITH	Turners Choice	130a.	3 - 2
ELIJAH SMITH	Cannan 15a. London 15a. Cannan 200a. Goshan 46a. unknown 17a.	293a.	3 - 3
JANNITTE SMITH	Bucks Neck	150a.	3 - 1
JOHN SMITH	Alderbury 150a. Addn. to Folly 20½a. Gum Ridge 40a. Good Luck 20a. ___? Lott 36a.	266a.	2 - 3
JOHN STURGIS	Friends Goodwill, Winders Addn. old Plantation 160a.	295a.	1 - 4
JOHN SMITH	(George Smith Security)		0 - 0
ARCHIBLAD SMITH	Bacon Quarter 100a. Shady Neck 200a. Tract of Forrest?150a.	450a.	3 - 4
BENJAMIN SAVAGE	End of Strife	200a.	0 - 0
Jo? SHOWELL	Enlargement 60a. Conclusion 121a.	181a.	0 - 0

PHILLIP QUINTON, assessor of WICOMICO 100

OWNERS NAME	LAND	TOTAL ACRES	WHITE INHAB. MALE-FEMALE
ELIJAH SHOCKLEY	Conclusion 291a. Naboth Vineyard 81a. Shockleys Priviledge 27a. Shockleys Choice 81a. Addition to R___ 49a.	529a.	4 - 4
SAUL SHOCKLEY	Conclusion 125a. Bacon Quarter 234a. Myrtle Grove 50a.	309a.	5 - 4
NATHANIEL SMULLING	Duncastle	72a.	4 - 4
RANDAL SMULLEN	pt. Supply 170a. Smullens Meadow 16a. Riggins Content	191a.	2 - 3
JOHN COOKSEY	Green Meadow	40a.	3 - 3
SHADRACK CROUCH	none		3 - 3
NATHAN CULVER	unknown 80a.and half of saw mill 25a.	105a.	1 - 2
JOHN CULVER	Mill Lott & half of saw mill 65a. Purkins Chance 150a.	215a.	2 - 2
MARGUERITTE CAREY	Careys Folly	50a.	4 - 2
LEVIN CAREY of L.	(Levin Carey Security)		0 - 0
DAVID CATHELL	Cathells Centure 50a. Davids Addn. 50a. Fooks Cost 100a.	300a.	2 - 3
LEVI CATHELL	Fooks Cost 100a.	100a.	2 - 1
JONATHAN CATHELL	(James Perdue Security)		0 - 0
JOHN CATHELL	Cathells Hardship 150a. Long Acre 80a. Mill Lot and Mill 11a. Safeguard 167a. James Additio n 24a.	532a.	1 - 3
ADAM CHRISTOPHER	Magdalens Choice 71a. Adams Venture 30a. White Clay 30a. unknown 50a.	181a.	4 - 3
NATHAN CULVER	Collins Addn.(living in Somerset County)	200a.	0 - 0
SUSANNAH CHRISTOPHER	none		1 - 3
DANIEL CATHELL	Safegurard 100a. Driskills Folly 50a.	150a.	2 - 3
PATRICK CAUSEY	Duncastle 134a. Peace & Plenty 25a.	159a.	6 - 4
MATHIAS CHRISTOPHER	Safeguard 337a. Mathias Addn. 50a. Dennis Addn.100a.	487a.	3 - 2
JONATHAN CAREY	none		5 - 3
THOMAS COX	Davis Choice	50a.	0 - 1
SARAH CARMAN	none		0 - 0
THOMAS CARBERRY	Dashiels Hazzard	388a.	1 - 2
ANN CHRISTOPHER	none		0 - 0
HEZEKIAH CAREY	Careys Hardship 69a. Shockleys Conclusion 42a. Black Harbour 50a. Hog Quarter 20a.	181a.	3 - 1
LEVIN CAREY of Thomas,	Security 33a. Conclusion 50a. Carreys Lott 54a. Safeguard 50a. Careys Choice 50a.	237a.	3 - 1
JOHN DAVIS	Scandown 300a. Castlefire 52a. Adventure 45a. Davis Lott 25a. Hogyard??Quarter 16a.	438a.	5 - 4
JOHN SHOCKLEY	Shockleys Security 60a.	60a.	3 - 1
PHILLIP SCROGIN	none		1 - 3

Phillip Quinton, assessor of WICOMICO 100

OWNERS NAME	LAND	TOTAL ACRES	White Inhab. MALE-FEMALE
ELIZABETH SHOCKLEY	Choice 100a. Addn to 56a. Knavery 50a.	256a.	3 - 2
STEPHEN STANFORD	Driskills Industry	37a.	5 - 5
ROBERT STANFORD	Winders Addition	52a.	1 - 1
SARAH SEADY	Sarahs Choice	50a.	2 - 1
JOSHUA STURGIS Jr.	New Holland 103a. Hungary Quarter 70a. Cox's Choice 100a.	273a.	1 - 3
JOSHUA STURGIS Sr.	Safeguard 123a. Mannor land 309a.	432a.	3 - 5
ZADOCK TURNER	Turners Delight	50a.	0 - 0
JAS. TRADER	Davis Choice 30a. McGees Lott 200a.	230a.	2 - 4
LEAH THOMPSON	Preston 300a. & Addn. to 25a. Come by Chance 50a.	375a.	1 - 4
LEVIN TURNER	Plumpton Salt Ash	100a.	2 - 3
SOUTHY TIGNAL	WInders Addition	100a.	3 - 5
JOHN TAYLOR Jr.	Jones Delight 65a. Security 100a.	165a.	3 - 4
JACOB TULL	Little Profit	50a.	4 - 4
JOHN TOADVINE	none		3 - 1
SAMUEL TOWNSEND	Smiths Choice 50a. Smiths Ending 50a. Holders Folly 129a.	229a.	4 - 4
JOHN TAYLOR Sr.	Taylors Purchase	50a.	2 - 3
WILLIAM TWIGGS	none		2 - 1
ARNOLD TOADVINE	Henrys Mill 70a. Oak Ridge 30a. Henrys Hardship 41a. Toadvines Choice 49a. Ditto 20a. Slim Chance 39a.	249a.	1 - 0
PETER TAYLOR	none		1 - 1
MARY TOADVINE	Henrys Choice 107a. Toadvines Hardship 44a. Strife 4½a. Long Axre 6a.	161½a.	4 - 2
ELIAS TAYLOR	(Elisha Parker Security)		0 - 0
STEPHEN TOADVINE	Summerfield 100a. Hard Luck 30a. Dunkirk 50a. Magdalenes Choice 19a.	199a.	2 - 4
HENRY TOADVINE	Toadvines Hard Luck	44a.	2 - 3
WILLIAM TOADVINE	Good Luck 100a. Long Acre 50a. Toadvines Hard Luck 6a.	156a.	1 - 0
MARY TWIGG	none		0 - 3
SAMUEL TURNER	none		1 - 2
JOHN VENABLES	Poor Chance	50a.	0 - 0
MATHIAS VINSON	Hobbses Mischance	79a.	2 - 3
GEORGE DAVIS	Runy Ridge 50a. Penditch?	100a.	5 - 4
SARAH DISHROON	none		2 - 4
JOSIAH DENNIS	Saw Mill Supply 50a. High Ridge 397a. Parkers Support 40a.	487a.	2 - 3
STEPHEN DIKES	Saw Mills Supply 50a. High Ridge 397a. Parkers Support 40a. Dikes Attempt 50a.	537a.	3 - 3
SPENCER DAVIS	none		3 - 4
SAUL DAVIS	Davis Neck	110a.	2 - 1

Phillip Quinton, assessor of WICOMICO 100

OWNERS NAME	LAND	TOTAL ACRES	White Inhab. MALE-FEMALE
WILLIAM DALEY	Davis's Choice	50a.	0 - 0
SHADRICK DRISKILL	none		3 - 5
MOSES DRISCOLL Sr.	Kings Lott	225a.	4 - 3
MOSES DRISKILL Jr.	Safeguard	102a.	3 - 3
DANIEL DIKES	Dikes Security & Dikes Dispute	306a.	3 - 4
AMBROSE DIXON	Dixons Green	293a.	1 - 2
OUTERBRIDGE DIXON	Dixons Green 150a. Thorntons Folly 13a.	163a.	2 - 2
NABOTH DIKES	none		4 - 2
NATHANIEL DIXON	Dixons Good Luck 250a. Dixons Green 57a. Dixons Conclusion 33a.	340a.	4 - 3
WILLIAM DRISKELL Sr.	none		1 - 2
JOHN DRISKILL	none		5 - 4
ADAM DRISKILL	(Jno Driskel Security)		0 - 0
ELGAGE DRISKILL	Kings Sale	147a.	6 - 4
SAMUEL DAVIS	Golden Quarter 100a. Security	173a.	0 - 0
GOERGE DISHEROON	Comeby Chance 73a. Manor land 123a.	196a.	5 - 5
JOHN DASHIELL Jr.	Dixons Green 140a. Dixons Green 75a.		1 - 6
WILLIAM DIKES	Williams Venture 220a. Williams Choice 50a.	270a.	4 - 6
PATIENCE DAVIS	Refor 100a. Poormans Chance 25a. Bottle Ridge 5a.	130a.	1 - 1
JOSHUA DORMAN	none		1 - 1
Col. JOSEPH DASHIELL	New Holland 250a. Ditto renewed 150a. Arrabich 75a. Pole Hammilton 100a. Fathers advice 50a. Mcrigolante 493a. Security 100a. Mill Lot, Dikes Choice, Middle Lott 400a. Nelsons Meadow 22½a. Mill dam & Mills 20a.	1660½a.	2 - 2
(for Hast Handy)	Mill Lott 9a. Handys Frolick 5a. Rim Ridge 260a. Handys Security 350a. Poormans Hope & Discovery 80a. Handys Outlett 50a.	704a.	
(for Moses Claywell)	Lamp 150a. Smiths Histry 195a. Smiths Last Choice 40a.	385a.	
WILLIAM VENSON	young man -none		0 - 1
TABITHA VANCE	none		1 - 3
WILLIAM WILLIS	Good Luck	50a.	2 - 3
BENJAMIN WILLIS	none		3 - 3
NATHANIEL WHALEY	Arabia 75a. Lingos Outlett 50a. Hazzard 13a. Surplus Land 100a.	238a.	3 - 4
WILLIAM WILSON	Griffins Chance 50a. Little Addition 27a.	77a.	5 - 4
JAMES WARD(Sussex)	Second Choice	110a.	0 - 0
WILLIAM WINDER	unknown	400a.	0 - 0
BENJAMIN WAILES	Security	73a.	1 - 3
BOAZ WALSTON	Cannaan 75a. Canada 40a. Friends Present 10a.	125a.	4 - 2

Phillip Quinton, assessor of WICOMICO 100

OWNERS NAME	LAND	TOTAL ACRES	White Inhab MALE-FEMALE
JONATHAN PARSONS	Parsons Conquest 490a. Camp 50a.	540a.	3 - 4
LEVIN PARSONS	(Jonathan Parsons Security		1 - 0
LEAH PERDUE	New Holland renewed	80a.	3 - 2
JAMES PERDUE Sr.	James Choice 50a.	50a.	1 - 1
JOHN PERDUE Jr.	none		1 - 2
GEORGE PERDUE of Jos.	none		2 - 1
WILLIAM POLLITT	Hold Fast 500a. Chestneut Ridge 152a.	552a.	1 - 0
SAMUEL POLLITT	none		1 - 0
JON a. POLLITT	Sandy Hill	200a.	0 - 0
WILLIAM PARSONS	Williams Adventure 194a. Double Purchase 50a. Benjamins Security 81a. Jas. Purchase 25a. Forrest Grove 25a. Williams Choice 50a. Addn. to Wm.'s Choice 250a. Parsons Conquest 10a. Good Increase 67a.	752a.	3 - 4
SAMUEL POPE	none		4 - 1
SAMUEL PARSONS	none		1 - 2
ELISHA PARKER Sr.	Parkers Delight 220a. ditto Last Choice 54a. Bacon Quarter 430a. Parkers Mistake 50a. Handys Beginning 50a.	794a.	2 - 4
George Perdue of George,	none		2 - 1
SARAH PUCKUM	none		0 - 1
ELISHA PARKER Jr.	(Elisha Parker Security)		1 - 0
JACOB PARKER	Jacobs Industry 27a. Parkers Chance 50a. ditto Security 50a. Aberdeen 50a. Bacon Quarter 342a.	519a.	4 - 3
GEORGE PARKER of Elisha,	none		2 - 1
SOLOMON CLAYWELL	none		3 - 3
GEORGE POLLITT	Poverty Neck 200a. Unknown	440a.	0 - 0
ALLEN QUINN	Myrtle Ridge 37½a. Cherry Hill 200½a.	237½a.	0 - 0
JOHN ROBERTS	Rapho	100a.	0 - 0
CHARLES ROACH	Security	50a.	1 - 2
ELIZABETH ROBINSON	Riggins Content	30a.	0 - 3
JOSEPH RIGGS	Haymans Hardship	52a.	3 - 3
ELIZABETH ROOKE	Covingtons Chance	60a.	3 - 2
JAMES ROACH	Summerfield 150a. Good Luck	175a.	2 - 8
THOMAS MURRAY	___Milnnum	50a.	1 - 1
STEPHEN MITCHELL	none		1 - 4
SUSANNAH MURFEE	none		2 - 2
EDWARD McGLAMERY	(Saul Davis Security)		1 - 0
RUBIN McGEE	Dormans Chance	106a.	5 - 2
RICHARD MILLS	Cox's Choice 36a. Manor land 122a.	158a.	3 - 5
ALEXANDER MADDUX	(hezekiah Maddux Security)		0 - 0
EDMUND N. NELMS	Kirkminster	225a.	2 - 2
JOHN NELMS Jr.	Safeguard 94a. Buck Ridge 100a. Williams Adventure 100a. Castle Fine 240a. Cax's Advice 150a. New England 100a. Hog Quarter 30a. Hobbs Choice 70a. Garden Spot 25a.	918a.	0 - 0

Phillip Quinton, assessor of WICOMICO 100

OWNERS NAME	LAND	TOTAL ACRES	White Inhab. MALE-FEMALE
MATTHEW OLLIPHANT	Joseph____?	67a.	2 - 3
SPENCER OWINS	none		1 - 2
JOSHUA OWINS	Joshuas Choice	90a.	2 - 2
CHARLES PHILLIPS HILL, Jr.	Long Acre 70a. Addition 201a.	271a.	1 - 2
GOERGE PARSONS	Friends Denial 150a. Addition 133a. Conclusion 100a. McGees Lott 63a.	446a.	4 - 5
JORDAN PARSONS	(George Parsons Security)		1 - 0
JOHN PARKER of Geo.	Cherrystone Lott and Alderberry	150a.	6 - 6
JAMES PERDUE	Hyprocits Deceived	50a.	2 - 2
ISAAC PHILLIPS	Goshen 150a. Florada 100a.	250a.	6 - 2
MOSES PANK	none		1 - 1
JACOB PHILLIPS	Gordys Delight	100a.	1 - 1
JACOB PHILLIPS Jr.	(Joseph Dennis Security)		0 - 0
JOHN PARKER	none		2 - 3
JOHN PHILLIPS	none		2 - 3
ALEXANDER PORTER	Addition 50a. Myrtle Grove 90a. Cathels Chance 70a.	210a.	6 - 3
THOMAS PRUITT	Mt. Pleasant	50a.	4 - 3
JAMES PERDUE of John,	Benjamins Choice 22½a. Holly Grove 13½a. Forrest Grove 50a. Myrtle Grove 50a. Perdues Luck 50a. Point Lookout 22½a.	208a.	5 - 3
JOHN PERDUE Sr.	End of Strife 65a. Eagle Point 155a. Beaver Dam 50a. Security 150a.	420a.	2 - 4
BENJAMIN JOHNSON	Safeguard 153a. Williams Choice 50a.	203a.	4 - 4
COMFORT JAMES	James Choice	24a.	1 - 1
FRANCIS LANK	none		0 - 0
SOLOMON LAYFIELD	White Oak Swamp	50a.	3 - 2
BENJAMIN LEONARD	New Providence	52½a.	1 - 1
WILLIAM LAYFIELD	Layfields Chance 50a. Baron Ridge 25a. Long Wait 100a.	175a.	2 - 2
GEORGE LOW	New Holland	50a.	2 - 0
ROBERT LAYFIELD	Davis's Choice	50a.	0 - 0
JOHN LAMBERSON	Bald Cypress Venture	80a.	1 - 1
SARAH LAYFIELD	none		3 - 1
THOMAS LOW	none		3 - 2
JOHN LOKEY	Safeguard	133a.	5 - 5
SARAH LIVINGSTON	Abraham Lott	125a.	1 - 3
TOD LIVINGSTON	(Stephen Horsey Security)		0 - 0
THOMAS LAYFIELD	Supply	91a.	1 - 2
JOHN LAYFIELD	Supply	80a.	1 - 5
HEZEKIAH MADDUX	Security Enlarged	236a.	2 - 7
JOHN MEARS	Eden 100a. Propiety 50a.	150a.	2 - 2
DANIEL MELSON Sr.	Stephens Security 70a. Peters Choice 30a. Gad o Hopes 87a. Melsons Addition 50a. Addn. to Good Hope 45a. Hog Range 61a.	343a.	1 - 1
DANIEL MELSON Jr.	Hearns Addition	70a.	0 - 0
JOHN McNAB	none		1 - 1

Phillip Quinton, assessor of WICOMICO 100

OWNERS NAME	LAND	TOTAL ACRES	White Inhab. MALE-FEMALE
WILLIAM McBRIDE	Addn. to Frustration 50a. Jona. Choice 27a. Causeys Adventure 115a. Board Tree Swamp 232a. Quason 100a. Williams Chance 129a.	703a.	2 - 6
JOSIAH McGEE	none		2 - 4
DAVID McGEE	New Holland	50a.	3 - 4
WILLIAM MILLS	New Holland	75a.	4 - 4
JOHN MUNGAR	Minnium	50a.	1 - 5
JACOB MORRIS	Collins Chance	132a.	1 - 1
JOSHUA MORRIS	Measleys Beginning & Collins Chance	124a.	1 - 1
JOHN McGEE	Conclusion	116a.	3 - 1
DAVIS McGEE	Shockleys Security	130a.	4 - 4
JOSHUA MADDOX	none		5 - 2
MARY MORRIS	Collins Chance	62a.	1 - 1
PRISCILLA MUNGAR	Minnium	50a.	4 - 3
MARY HOWARD	none		1 - 3
ISAAC HAYMAN	Adleys Chance 50a. Fatters Quarter 50a.	100a.	3 - 3
CHARLES HAYMAN	Hopewell	104a.	3 - 2
EBENEZER HANDY	Handys Beginning 250a. Worcester side 70a. Good Luck 20a.	340a.	2 - 5
JOHN HILL	none		1 - 2
JACOB HATHE	Nibletts Point	50a.	2 - 1
SMITH HATHE	Haths Venture 95a. Lingos Priviledge 11a.	106a.	4 - 5
JOSHUA HOLLOWAY	unknown	300a.	2 - 5
MICAJAH HANDCOCK	none		7 - 7
JOHN HARRISON	none		3 - 2
SAMUEL HORSEY	none		0 - 0
JOHN HARRIS HAYMAN	Pettitts Chance	25a.	0 - 0
JAMES HAYMAN	Hopewell	49a.	1 - 1
CHARLES HAYMAN Jr.	Hopewell	64a.	5 - 2
MARGARET HAYMAN	Fatters Quarter 96a. Haymans Outlett 50a.	146a.	2 - 1
RACHEL HAYMAN	Fatters Quarter 39a. Haymans Addn. 15a. Pettits Chance 75a.	129a.	0 - 4
STEPHEN HORSEY	Brothers Goodwill 50a. Abrahams Lott	175a.	1 - 1
SMITH HORSEY	Horseys Fackaboss	757a.	0 - 0
WILLIAM HOLLAND	Fackabus	200a.	4 - 2
WILLIAM HORSEY	Domain Chance 100a. Manor Land 400a.	500a.	0 - 0
(for brother Isaac)	New Holland 75a. with mills, Outlett 50a.	125a.	
NICHOLAS HAYMAN	Safeguard 91a. Fern Ridge 50a.	141a.	1 - 2
MATHIAS HOBBS	Geo.s' Lott 211a. Hobbs Adventure 63a.	274a.	0 - 0
SPENCER HARRIS	Cornhill 51a. Porters Beginning 50a. Givans Liberty 129a.	230a.	0 - 0
BENJAMIN HENSON	Hensons Addition	40a.	0 - 0

PHILLIP QUINTON, Assessor of WICOMICO 100

OWNERS NAME	LAND	TOTAL ACRES	White Inhab. MALE-FEMALE
Dr. JAMES HOUSTON	Tulls Knavery 95a. Covingtons Choice 161a. Pembroke 50a. Hickory Ridge 50a. Good increase 30a.	386a.	0 - 0
MARY HALE	Addn. to Reading	131a.	1 - 2
JOHN HAYMAN	Flatt Ridge	40a.	0 - 0
JOHNSON HAYMAN	none		1. - 3
SAMUEL INGOLSON	Long Acre 100a. Long Chance 7a. Green Bryor 55a. Manor land 213a.	375a.	0 - 0
JOHN JAMES	Rebeccas Delight 50a. Round Hill 50a.		6 - 3
PURNELL JOHNSON	Hog Pen Ridge	61a.	1 - 0
CHASE?DORMAN	Quaikeson Neck	50a.	4 - 3
WILLIAM DYMOCK	Cox's ___ 165a. Nelms Neglect 30a. Safeguard 100a.	295a.	0 - 0
MOSES ELLIOTT	Hyprocits deceived	50a.	2 - 2
ADKINS DENNSI	none		3 - 3
ZADOCK ENNIS	DUNCASTLE 600a. Riggins content 33a.	650a.	1 - 5
JOHN FLINT	Friends Denial	150a.	2 - 0
JOSHUA FREENY	unknown	41a.	3 - 6
JESSE FOOKS	Duncastle 620a. Addn. to Exchange 126a.	746a.	6 - 2
WILLIAM FREENY	none		1 - 1
THOMAS FOOKS	Fort Neck 200a. Long Acre 121a. Fooks Cost 21a. Fort Neck 50a.	392a.	3 - 3
MARY FOOKS	Long Acre 100a. Fooks Lott	192a.	1 - 2
WILLIAM FOOKS	Summer Pasture 115a. Bacon Quarter 20a.	135a.	1 - 2
JOHN FREENY	Chance 32½a. Parkers Support 25a. Florada 230a.	297½a.	0 - 0
ROUND GIVAN	Florada	200a.	0 - 0
FRANCIS GURLEY	none		0 - 1
SOLOMON GIVANS	Corn Hill 51a. Givans liberty 79a.	130a.	3 - 3
JOSEPH GLADDING	none		2 - 2
WILLIAM GIBB	(Levin Smith Security)		0 - 0
JOHN GORDY	Hyprocits Deceaved 150a. Brandy Ridge 45a. Parkers Mistake 50a.	295a.	0 - 0
WILLIAM GORDY	Peters Choice	100a.	3 - 1
PETER GORDY	Gordys Chance 100a. Addn. to Chance 25a. Gordys Adventure 25a. Parkers Hard Fortune 113a. Parkers Addition 25a. High Ridge 25a. Brandy Ridge 25a. Peters Chance 195a. Addition to Milford 143a.	686a.	3 - 5
WILLIAM GREER	none		2 - 2
ELIJAH HERON	Doe Park 50a. Buck Ridge 50a. Laughable 50a.	150a.	5 - 5
ROBERT HANDY	none		1 - 2
JOHN HERON	Lightwood Ridge 34a. First Choice 40a. Smiths Lot 60a. Addn. to Smiths Lot 40a.	174a.	1 - 2

Phillip Quinton, assessor of WICOMICO 100

OWNERS NAME	LAND	TOTAL ACRES	White Inhab. MALE-FEMALE
JOHN HALL	Winter Quarter	50a.	3 - 3
CHARLES HARRIS	Alderbury	200a.	3 - 4
SAMUEL HERON	Cape Britten 100a. Methvens Chance 50a.	150a.	0 - 0

Isaac Houston, assessor for SNOW HILL 100.

JOSEPH BISHOP	young man		1 - 0
JAMES BENNETT	½ lott 9, lot 10		5 - 3
Dr. SMITH BISHOP	1/3 lot 3 1/3 lot 34		0 - 0
LEVIN BLAKE	for Atkinsons heirs pt. Lot 12		0 - 0
SAMUEL COX	none		3 - 1
ANDREW CATHERWOOD	none		1 - 0
JOHN CHAMBERS	Lots 25 & 26		2 - 1
ELIZABETH CURREN	none		1 - 1
JOSHUA DUER	½ Lott 9		5 - 4
MITCHELL DOWNES	1 lott		5 - 2
MITCHELL DOWNES	1 lott		5 - 2
JAMES DUER	1/3 Lott 9		2 - 1
ROBERT DENNIS Esq.	2 lots		2 - 1
NEHEMIAH DORMAN	lots 26 & 29		11 - 2
ELEANOR FASSITT	1/8 Lott 12		1 - 3
PHILIP GUTHERIE	none		4 - 2
JOHN GUNN	½ lott and 1 lott		7 - 4
JAMES GIVANS	2 lots		3 - 1
SAMUEL GUNN	none		0 - 0
ELIZABETH HANDY	pt. Lot 12		3 - 2
Capt. WM. HANDY	for Whittingtons heirs Lot 7		0 - 0
JONATHAN HUTCHISON	½ lot N		7 - 4
SARAH HAYWARD	lot 4		0 - 0
ROBERT HENRY	lot N		0 - 0
MATHIAS HANDY	young man		0 - 0
JOHN HUDSON	1 lot		4 - 2
LUKE HOPKINS	1/3 Lot 11		1 - 5
JOHN SCARBOROUGH	1 lot N		0 - 0
ELEANOR STEVENS	lots 14 & 15		0 - 0
WALTER SMITH	lots 51 & 53		4 - 5
JOSHUA TOWNSEND	lots 70 & 11		0 - 0
MAJOR TOWNSEND	¼ Lot 11		0 - 0
JEREMIAH TOWNSNED	1/6 lot 12		0 - 0
GEORGE TRUITT	lots 51 & 52		3 - 1
HENRY TRUITT	for John Spence ½ lot 5		0 - 0
HANNAH WEBB	none		1 - 2
PATRICK WATERS	lot 6		0 - 0
PETER WHITE	lot 6a.		1 - 1
WILLIAM WATERS	½ lot 11		3 - 6
WILLIAM WISE	lot 29		4 - 4
ARALANTER HOPKINS	none		0 - 2
BERRYMAN HAYWARD	½ lot 13		1 - 5
JOSEPH KILLAM	young man		0 - 0
JAMES LeCOUNT	lots 75 & 76		4 - 2
ROBERT LAMBDEN	½ lot 3		0 - 0
LEVIN LONG	2 lots		0 - 0
JAMES MARTIN	lot N. ½ lot & 5lots Snow Hill 15 for William Handy		3 - 6

ISAAC HOUSTON, assessor for SNOW HILL 100

OWNERS NAME	LAND	TOTAL ACRES	White Inhab. MALE-FEMALE
Pollis? MARTIN	1 lot N		0 - 0
VANCE MARTIN	1 Not N		0 - 0
JOHN MURRAY	young man		0 - 0
WILLIAM MORRIS	lot 2		0 - 0
THOMAS MARTIN of James, young man			0 - 0
JOHN MULLING	1/16 Lot 12		1 - 2
JOHN MARTIN	1 lot P.		0 - 0
JOHN MARTIN of George, none			0 - 0
SAMUEL NELSON	young man		0 - 0
JOHN NEILLE	for Morrises heirs Lot N		2 - 1
THOMAS PRICE	none		2 - 2
ROBERT P. YELVERTON	2 lots		0 - 0
McKEMMY PORTER	¼ lot		3 - 2
BENJAMIN PURNELL	lot 35		0 - 0
PHILLIP QUINTON	2 lots		0 - 0
GEORGE ROBINSON	young man		0 - 0
THOMAS RANDALL	2 lots		4 - 2
ELIZABETH ROSS	1 lot N. 33½a. lot		2 - 1
BOWDEN ROBINS	1 lot		0 - 0
DANIEL ROBINS	1 lot		0 - 0
ELIJAH STURGIS	1 lot		3 - 4
JOHN SPENCE	½ lot		0 - 0
PARKER SELBY	young man		0 - 0
JOHN SELBY	1 lot		0 - 0
SAMUEL SNODY(Capt.)	lot 9		0 - 0
WILLIAM SELBY	¼ lot		3 - 3

Elisha Purnell Assessor of BOQUETENORTON 100

JOHN AYRES	Scarboroughs Lott 163a. Poplar Hill Enlarged 61a. Piney Purchase 200a.	424a.	1 - 1
ANN AKE	none		0 - 2
WILLIAM BISHOP	Hard Labour 12a. Selbys outlett	145a.	2 - 3
NATHANIEL BRATTEN	Brothers Choice 96a. Double Purchase 130a. Basten Stroke 50a. Albany 115a.	391a.	2 - 3
BENJAMIN BISHOP	(John Ayres Security)		0 - 0
BELITHA BRITTINGHAM	Poplar Ridge 70a. None Such 130a.	200a.	3 - 5
ELIZABETH BRITTINGHAM	none		0 - 1
THOMAS BRITTINGHAM	Dissappointment 3a. Poplar Ridge 112a. Paynters Fancy 50a.	165a.	1 - 2
JOSHUA BRITTINGHAM	none		1 - 0
EPHAMIA BRITTINGHAM	none		0 - 1
MARY BRITTINGHAM	Beckford 50a. Canadee 62a.	112a.	0 - 3
WILLIAM BRITTINGHAM	Beckford	210a.	2 - 2
WILLIAM BRITTINGHAM Jr.	none		2 - 1
SAMUEL BRATTEN	none		1 - 0
WILLIAM BISHOP Sr.	BasenStoke	200a.	8 - 2

Elisha Purnell, assessor of BOQUETENORTON 100

OWNERS NAME	LAND	TOTAL ACRES	White Inhab. MALE-FEMALE
SAMUEL BRITTINGHAM	Brittinghams Addition	50a.	1 - 2
JOHN BISHOP	Londonderry	66½a.	1 - 3
ELIZABETH BISHOP	Scarborough Castle	154a.	2 - 1
JESSE BENNETT	Patricks Hill	100a.	1 - 2
CHARLES BISHOP	Simpleton	100a.	2 - 3
JOHN BOWAN	none		3 - 1
SAMUEL BRADFORD	Mulberry Grove 145a. Morris Security 146a. Truitts Harbour 100a.	391a.	5 - 4
JOHN SELBY	Poplar Hill & Exon Enlarged 855a. Dumfreeze 46 3/4a. Ship yard 24a.	925¾a.	0 - 0
ROUND TRUITT	MulberryGrove	76a.	1 - 2
WILLIAM TRUITT	Truitts Harbour 175½a. ditto 95a.	270½a.	5 - 3
EDWARD TRUITT	none		1 - 2
JACOB TEAGUE	Spauldin 100a. Scotland 23a.	123a.	1 - 2
ILI TRUITT	Truitts Harbor	95a.	2 - 2
JOHN TARR	Mulberry Grove	38a.	2 - 3
KENDAL TAYLOR	none		1 - 0
RICHARD TAYLOR	Scarborough Castle 50a. unknown 1a.	51a.	2 - 4
MAJOR TOWNSEND	Halls Discovery	195a.	4 - 3
WILLIAM TARR	Rochester	100a.	5 - 1
JOSHUA TOWNSEND Esq.	Salem 200a. Dumfreeze 156a. Water Lott 56a. Snow Hill 1a.	413a.	4 - 3
PATRICK WATERS	Rochester	230a.	1 - 0
WILLIAM WEST	none		1 - 0
ELIZABETH WYANTS	none		1 - 2
ZADOCK WRIGHT	Chance 359½a. New Fairfield 900a. Spaulden 79a. Puzzle 33a. Fairfield 50a. Rich____? 300a.	1721a.	3 - 3
JESSE WATERS	none		2 - 2
LITTLETON ROBINS	Robins Folly	371a.	1 - 0
SHADRACK RICHARDSON	Smiths 1st. Choice 2a. Chance 8a. Dover 195a.	205a.	1 - 2
LEVI RICHARDSON	Mt.Ephraim	239½a.	1 - 5
ROBERT RICHARDSON Sr.	Mt.Ephraim 151a. part ditto 200a.	351a.	3 - 4
ROBERT RICHARDSON Sr.	none		1 - 1
ROBERT RICHARDSON	none		2 - 1
CHARLES RICHARDSON	none		3 - 5
WILLIAM RICHARDSON	none		4 - 4
ROBERT SCHOOLFIEDL	Jones Adventure 150a. Smiths 1st. Choice 156a.	306a.	3 - 1
JOHN SAVAGE	none		2 - 4
CHARLES SAWYER	none		2 - 2
ADAM STEPHENSON	London Derry	90a.	1 - 3
MATTHEW STEEL	Simpleton 426a. Durham house 30a.	456a.	3 - 1
JOHN SCARBOROUGH	Scarborough Castle 500a. Finis 50a.	550a.	5 - 2
Capt.GEORGE SPENCE	Mt Ephraim 290a. Privildge	360a.	4 - 4

Elisha Purnell, assessor of BOQUETENORTON 100

OWNERS NAME	LAND	TOTAL ACRES	White Inhab. MALE-FEMALE
JAMES STEEL	Dover 153a. Chance & Smiths 1st. Choice 40a.	193a.	0 - 0
SAMUEL SCARBROOUGH	Scarboroughs Castle	325a.	4 - 4
KENDAL SCARBROUGH	none		1 - 0
JOHN STURGIS	Rochester 140a. Sturgis's Chance & Double Purchase 96a.	206a.	2 - 3
ZADOCK STURGIS	none		1 - 0
ESTHER STEVENSON	none		2 - 3
JAMES STEVENSON	Rochester	200a.	3 - 2
MARGARET SPENCE	Piney Street 200a. Double Purchase 3a. Peru 70a.	273a.	0 - 2
ELIZABETH SPENCE	none		0 - 1
DAVID SPRING	none		1 - 2
HANNAH SELBY	Mardike	133a.	1 - 2
JOHN STEVENSON	Brattans Choice 112a. Johns industry 50a.	162a.	4 - 4
WILLIAM SPIERS	Simpleton	500a.	3 - 3
JOHN SPENCE	Smiths 1st. Choice 225a. Dover 105a. Chance 60a. Rattlesnake island 1a. Conveniency Addn. 77a. Salem 5a. Shaftsberry 5a. Littleworth 31a. Mardike 10a.	519a.	0 - 0
LEVI MERRILL	Patricks Hill 100a. Simpleton 90a. Reserve 19a. Mardike 262½a. Purnells Inheritance 229a. Patricks Choice 70a. Mt. Ephraim Partnership 194a. Londonderry 36a.	1050a.	4 - 3
Col. JAMES MARTIN	Dumfrieze	75a.	0 - 0
JAMES MORRIS	Mulberry Grove & Rochester	500a.	1 - 1
JOHN McCALLY	Spauldin	100a.	2 - 2
SACKER PARKER	Cannanree	195a.	3 - 4
WILLIAM PURNELL	Fairfields 200a. Fathers Care 65a. New Pharsalia 200a. Lots 1 & No.2 393a. Aarons Lott 50a. Poplar Ridge 17a. Beckford 3a.	928a.	6 - 4
WILLIAM PARKER	Smiths 1st. Choice 216½a. for Joseph Schoolfields heirs	216½a.	3 - 4
THOMAS PURNELL Sr.	Mt Ephraim 500a. Cow Quarter & Addn. to ditto 114a.	614a.	0 - 0
MARSHALL POYNTER	Dover	262a.	3 - 3
GEORGE PURNELL	Rochester 652a.	652a.	0 - 0
ROBERT YELVERTON	Flattberry	50a.	0 - 0
ELIJAH PEPPER	none		2 - 2
THOMAS POYNTER	none		5 - 1
ESTHER POLLITT	none		3 - 2
JOHN PURNELL	none		1 - 1
BENJAMIN PURNELL	Rochester	657a.	1 - 0
PHILLIP RAIN	none		3 - 1
ANN ROBINS	Fairfield 400a. Horn Hill Addn. & Waters Mill 106a. Fathers Care 50a. Double Purchase 200a. Baltimores Gift 250a. Londonderry 10a. Scotland 215a. Partnership 343a.	1368a.	3 - 5

Elisha Purnell, assessor of BOQUETENORTON 100

OWNERS NAME	LAND	TOTAL ACRES	White Inhab. MALE-FEMALE
THOMAS RICHARDSON	Mt. Ephraim	233½a.	1 - 0
	next page very poor and faded		
WILLIAM HOOK	none		3 - 3
SAMUEL HANDY	Conveneincy 200a. Hendersons Discovery 70a. Brandy Point 71a. St. Lawrence Neck 411a. 50a. unknown 50a. C____? enlarged 27a.	829a.	0 - 0
RALPH HOUSTON	Middle More Enlarged	371a.	5 - 2
ISAAC HOUSTON	Purnells Security 223a. unknown 37a.	260a.	0 - 0
CHARLES HENDERSON	unknown		1 - 0
BISHOP HENDERSON	unknown		1 - 0
JESSE HUGHES	none		1 - 0
JESSE? HENDERSON	Friendship 40a. unknown 219	259¾a.	3 - 2
WILLIAM HANDY	Handys Wharf	100a.	3 - 2
JOHN JOHNSON	unknown	50a.	3 - 3
LABAN JOHNSON	none		1 - 0
ISAAC MORRIS	none		5 - 3
MARGARET MUMFORD	none		0 - 1
JESSE MUMFORD	none		0 - 0
ELIZABETH MARCHMENT			2 - 3
GEORGE MUMFORD	none		1 - 3
PHILLIP MARSH	none		2 - 2
MAJOR MUMFORD	none		3 - 2
THOMAS MARTIN	Brotherhood, Martins Outlett ___ Luck & 203a. & 60a.	350+ a.	3 - 2
RHODA COSTON	none		3 - 5
HANNAH CHRISTOPHER	none		0 - 2
ELIZABETH CHRISTOPHER	none		0 - 1
JOB CLAYWELL	Durham House	159a.	5 - 2
MOSES CLAYWELL	(Job Claywell Security)		1 - 0
THOMAS COTTINGHAM	Double Purchase 7½a. Rochester 27½a.		2 - 6
FREDERICK CONNER	Durham House	75a.	1 - 2
WILLIAM CAMPBELL	Rochester	74½a.	4 - 4
SIMON COLLICK (negro)	Spences Venture 100a. Conviencies Addn. 12a.	112a.	0 - 0
GEORGE DENNIS	Flatbury	75a.	2 - 1
SAMUEL DREADON	none		2 - 1
MOSES DREADON	none		2 - 1
ELIZABETH DEVORIX	Baston Stroke 120a. Deverix Addition	187a.	1 - 1
JOHN DEVORIX	Rochester	190a.	1 - 1
WILLIAM DREADON	Parkers Adventure	75a.	2 - 3
JOHN DREADON	Parkers Adventure	225a.	4 - 3
LEVIN DAVIS	Carnade 12a. Mentmore 199a. Spauldin 76a.	287a.	5 - 5
EDWARD DAVIS	Friends Exchange	120a.	3 - 2
NEHEMIAH DORMAN	Markike	267a.	5 - 2
FRANCES DIXON	none		1 - 3
JOSHUA ENNIS	Flattery	100a.	0 - 0
NATHANIEL ENNIS	Edwards Lott	85a.	1 - 2

Elisha Purnell, assessor of BOQUETENORTON 100

OWNERS NAME	LAND	TOTAL ACRES	White Inhab. MALE-FEMALE
JOSEPH ENNIS	fern hall 164a. Fox's Harbour 24a. Edwards Lott 56a.	244a.	1 - 1
CORNELIUS ENNIS Jr.	Cannarnee 241a. Wild goose 30a.		
ELIZABETH EVANS, widow,	Summerfield	60a.	3 - 3
JACOB GRAY	Scarborough Castle	113a.	2 - 1
JOHN GRIER?	none		3 - 3
JOHN GORNWELL	Dover	100a.	3 - 5
ISAAC HAMMOND Sr.	none		1 - 1
JOHN HAILES	none		4 - 4

POCOMOKE 100

This portion of the film is very poor and some impossible to read

OWNERS NAME	LAND	TOTAL ACRES	MALE-FEMALE
HANNAH BACON	Chuckaluck	1000a.	5 - 4
ANDREW BROWN	Browns Purchase 30a. Amith 30a.	60a.	2 - 2
FRANCIS BRITT	Carters Discovery	100a.	4 - 3
WILSON BROWN	Addition	133½a.	4 - 3
THOMAS BENSTON	Addition to Discovery	243a.	0 - 0
JOSHUA BUTLER	none		2 - 2
BENJAMIN BUTLER	Nod.45a. Golden Purchase	125a.	5 - 3
WILLIAM BROWN	none		1 - 0
WILLIAM BALL	none		4 - 2
BETTY BETTS	none		2 - 1
WILLIAM COTTINGHAM	Coventry & pt.Saw Mill	200a.	2 - 3
JOHN COTTINGHAM	Old Head & Hanes Addn 141a. Warton 120a. 2/3 Saw mill	261a.	3 - 2
Joseph COTTINGHAM	(John Cottingham Security)		1 - 0
BETTE COTTINGHAM	none		0 - 3
WILLIAM CORBAN	Cypress Swamp 170a. Freemans Disocvery 30a. Greens Chance 100a. Mt. Hope 30a.	160a.	3 - 1
WILLIAM COTTINGHAM	Warton 7a. Addition Enlarged	54a.	4 - 3
BENNETT COPES	none		1 - 4
HAFTAR CLOGG	Flodders	30a.	2 - 1
EDMUND CROPPER	S____ Folly	170a.	3 - 5
EDWARD COVINGTON	Nicholas Choice 25a. Safeguard 70a. & unknown		5 - 4
PETER CHAILLE	Dispence 286¼a. Friends Security 29a.	315¼a.	0 - 0
THOMAS CLIFTON	none		2 - 1
WILLIAM CONNER	young man		1 - 0
STEPHEN DAIL	nonw		2 - 5
ROBERT DENNIS	West Swamp	244a.	0 - 0
A. DORMAN	none		1 - 2
SAMUEL DORMAN	Clainfasting	100a.	2 - 3
JOHN DORMAN	none		4 - 2
JOSIAH DICKERSON	Addition to Smiths Chance 445a. Donohoes Choice 175a.	620a.	5 - 6
JOHN DUKES	Lanes Discovery	50a.	3 - 2

OWNERS NAME	LAND	TOTAL ACRES	White Inhab. MALE-FEMALE
CORNELIUS DICKERSON	Whitley 157a. Limrick 40a. Cornelius Choice 9a. Security 100a.	306a.	5 - 1
JOSHUA DRYDEN	Dumfrieze	150a.	4 - 2
WILLIAM DUBBERLY	none		3 - 1
JOHN DRYDEN	Purkins Adventure 108a. Riggins Addn. 170a.	278a.	3 - 3
ABRAM DENSTON	Forrest	80a.	1 - 0
SARAH DENSTON of Isaac,	Choice	100a.	
LEVIN DENSTON	young man		1 - 0
SARAH DENSTON	Milesend	50a.	0 - 2
SARAH DENSTON of Phillip,	Riggins Addition 100a. Maidens Choice 50a.	150a.	1 - 3
ISABELA DENSTON	none		0 - 3
ELIZABETH DRUMMOND	Furnis's choice	100a.	0 - 5
JEMIMA TOWNSEND	Philadelphia 28a. New York 54a. Chance 68a. Delight and unknown 17a. 22a.	200+a.	1 - 3
JAMES TOWNSEND	of Danford,		2 - 1
CHARLES TOWNSEND	Security	89a.	3 - 3
SARAH TOWNSEND	Security	44a.	0 - 2
DANFORD TOWNSEND	unknown	40a.	2 - 3
ABSALOM TOWNSEND	Porters Discovery	65a.	1 - 0
EPHRAIM TOWNSEND	Porters Discovery	166a.	2 - 2
WILLIAM TILGHMAN	Townsends Choice 60a. Piney Grove 45a.	105a.	2 - 2
ANN TAYLOR	none		0 - 1
WILLIAM TOWNSEND	Porters Discovery	50a.	2 - 2
SAMUEL TILGHMAN	Porters Discovery	6a.	3 - 4
JEREMIAH TAYLOR	Forestland	50a.	4 - 3
SARAH TOWNSEND widow of Joseph,	none		0 - 3
ELIAS TOWNSEND	unknown	100a.	2 - 2
Jos. GRAY TAYLOR	Nod 102a. Basham 67a.	169a.	1 - 4
DENNIS TAYLOR	none		2 - 3
THEOPHILIUS TURNER	Furnis's Folly 50a.	50a.	0 - 0
MICHAEL VEASEY	Bacon Priviledge 62a. Exchange 60a.	122a.	1 - 1
HUGH VESTRY	Vestrys Purchase	20a.	1 - 3
SARAH WATSON	none		0 - 2
ELIZABETH WHITE	none		2 - 3
MAJOR WHITE	Benefield	345a.	3 - 2
WILLIAM WILLIS	none		1 - 0
JAMES WILLIAMS	Donohues Choice 172a. Dickinsons Discovery 177a.	349a.	3 - 4
JESSEE WATSON	Riggins Discovery	53a.	3 - 2
JAMES WONNELL	Golden Meadows 100a. WOnnells Choice 50a.	150a.	5 - 3
SAUL WARD	Mill Lott with grist Mill 15a. Hog Range 20a. Peru 30a.	65a.	0 - 0
JESSE WARD	unknown	50a.	0 - 0
JOHN WELLS	Riggins Addition	100a.	5 - 3
STEPHEN WHITE	Robins Hope 97a. Nicolas Choice 25a.	124a.	6 - 5

POCOMOKE 100

OWNERS NAME	LAND	TOTAL ACRES	White Inhab. MALE-FEMALE
WILLIAM WHITE	Robins Hope	131a.	5 - 3
JABEZ WILLIS	Donohoes Choice 150a. Johns Luck 37a. Donohoes Choice 10a.	197a.	4 - 5
PURNELL DRUMMOND	young man		1 - 0
MATTHEW DORMAN	Dormans Choice	50a.	4 - 4
ROBERT DUKES	Nancys Choice	155a.	2 - 3
CHARLES DONOHOE	none		3 - 2
SARAH DENSTON, widow of Charles,	none		0 - 2
SOLOMON ESHUM	Baylors adventure	100a.	2 - 2
JONATHAN ESHUM	none		2 - 4
DANIEL ESHUM	Eshums Last Choice	197a.	2 - 2
JONATHAN ESHUM	saw mill, no land		0 - 0
JOHN FLEMMING Jr.	Neighbors Goodwill 198a. Addition to Venture 127a. Second Choice 112a. Joshuas Ending 37a.	474a.	2 - 3
JOHN FLEMING Sr.	Addition to Centure 70a. Second Choice 362a.	432a.	2 - 4
JAMES GIBBS	LittleLott	100a.	1 - 0
ABRAM GIBBS	none		1 - 2
MOLLY GUTHREY	none		0 - 2
WILLIAM HANDY	Rich Isle 60a. (Balance unreadable		4 - 2
JOHAH HUDSON	none		2 - 3
LEVI HOLLAND	Ridge Discovery 240a.	240a.	5 - 4
JOHN HARRIS	none		1 - 1
Smith??HUNT	GRUBBY HILL	223a.	5 - 1
EDW.?HAMMOND	none		3 - 3
ALEC JOHNSON=	Beavans Choice 186a. Saw Mill supply 25a.	211a.	4 - 4
SAMUEL KELLY	none		4 - 3
THOMAS LANFORD	none		2 - 5
SARAH LAYFIELD	Donohoes Choice	25a.	3 - 2
JOHN LEONARD	Riggins Discovery	26a.	1 - 2
ROBT.LAMBDEN	(Henry Atkinson security)		1 - 0
DAVID LAYFIELD	none		1 - 3
THOMAS LOCKEY	Forrest land	25a.	6 - 2
WILLIAM McCUDDY	Thomas Selbys Purchase	185a.	4 - 3
MARCY MADDOX	Benefield	700a.	1 - 1
LAZARUS MADDUX	Flemings Purchase 45a. Poor & Honest 68a. Look Out 27a.	140a.	3 - 4
MATHIAS MILES	Heron Quarter & saw & grist mill,	50a.	0 - 0
ALEXANDER McALLEN	Support & Scotland	125a.	0 - 0
Capt.THOMAS MARTIN	Defiance & Security	201a.	0 - 0
GEORGE MARTIN	Defiance & Security	291a.	0 - 0
Col.J.MARTIN	Defiance & Security	291a.	0 - 0
ZOROBABLE MADDUX	Riggins Discovery	93 3/4a.	3 - 2
SOTHY NEWTON	none		2 - 3
MARY NOBLE	What you will	10a.	1 - 3
JAMES NOBEL	Exchange 31a. Houstons Lott 32a.	63a.	3 - 4

POCOMOKE 100

OWNERS NAME	LAND	TOTAL ACRES	White Inhab. MALE-FEMALE
EBE OUTTEN	none		0 - 0
JAMES OTWELL	Basham 36a. Riggins Discovery 43a.	79a.	2 - 2
LEVIN OWENS	none		2 - 1
JABEZ?OWENS	Owens Chance	37a.	5 - 4
PETER OWENS	Safeguard 100a. Owens Chance 50a.	150a.	3 - 2
ELIJAH POWELL	Williams Choice 30a. Addition 31a.	61a.	3 - 0
WILLIAM POWELL	none		2 - 1
GEORGE PEWSY	none		1 - 0
ISAAC PEWSY	Bacon Hill	130a.	1 - 0
L___ Pewsy	Puseys Choice 50a.	50a.	4 - 1
THOMAS PEWSY	Riggins Lott 200a. Addn. to Jo___? 260a.	460a.	0 - 0
JOHN POWELL	unknown		1 - 0
PHILLIP QUINTON	Phillips Addition 16a. Buck Ridge 300a.	316a.	5 - 0
JOSEPH RICHARDS	Atkinsons Conclusion 70a. Neighbors Mistake 42½a. Overtons Lott 191a. Bevans Overcome 200a.	513½a.	2 - 3
SARAH READ	none		0 - 2
SAMUEL ROBINS	none		3 - 0
A.___ RIGGIN	What you will	195 3/4a.	2 - 1
DARBY RIGGIN	What you will	50a.	1 - 0
JOHN RIGGIN	What you will	43a.	3 - 3
ELIZABETH RUARK	none		1 - 2
MARY RUARK	Cow Quarter 20a.	20a.	1 - 3
EZEKIEL RUARK	Turners Choice??	50a.	1 - 2
HEZEKIAH RUARK	none		4 - 1
CHARLES REDDING	none		1 - 0
LITTLETON RIGGIN	Forrest Lott	22a.	2 - 0
JOHN RUARK	none		5 - 2
SOUTHY ROACH	none		1 - 0
JAMES SELBY	Bonefield	100a.	2 - 1
JOHN SELBY	Bonefield	170a.	2 - 4
EZEKIEL SELBY	Bonefield	159a.	1 - 0
WILLIAM SELBY Jr.	Bonefield	189a.	2 - 2
JOHN SCOTT	none		2 - 0
JOSEPH SCOTT	none		2 - 0
JOSEPH TILGHMAN	Balance of page unreadable		
DORMAN TOWNSEND			
STEPHEN TOWNSEND			
T. TOWNSEND	none		
JAMES ATKINSON	Choice 180a. Choice 240a. unknown 100a.	520a.	4 - 4
THOMAS ATKINSON	none		1 - 0
WILLIAM ATKINSON	Choice 300a. Atkinsons Outlett 60a.	360a.	3 - 2
ANGELO ATKINSON	pt. Choice, = unknown		1 - 3
NATHAN ANDERSON	none		2 - 4
JOHN S. ALEXANDER	Flemings Discovery 30a. unreadable		2 - 3

POCOMOKE 100

OWNERS NAME	LAND	TOTAL ACRES	White Inhab. MALE-FEMALE
THOMAS ATKINSON	Thomas Choice 215a. +		2 - 3
WILLIAM ALLEN Esq.	unknown 226+	3 - 5	
JOHN BEVANS	Milton	100a.	1 - 3
SARAH BEVANS	none		0 - 3
THOMAS BARNES	Addition 50a. Caudrys Security 102a. Cypress Grove 18a. Townsends Discovery 180a.	350a.	3 - 1
ROWLAND BEVANS	unknown		4 - 3
WILLIAM BEVANS	unknown	200a.	6 - 4
JOHN BOWLAND	Wm. McCuddy Security		1 - 0
MARY BOWEN	Warton 158a.	158a.	3 - 3
WILLIAM BOWEN	Wharton ?		2 - 1

END OF WORCESTER COUNTY

INDEX

ABBOTT-ABBITT-23-24
ACWORTH-7-12-13
ADAMS-ADDAMS-1-13-24-33-43-
    46-51-73
AGNAFIELD-79
AIRES-AYRES-7-55-73-79-95
AKE-67-95
ALEXANDER-102
ALLIPHANT-85
ALLISON-67
AKEMAN-23
ALPHA-12
ALLEN-1-13-55-59-79-103
ANDERSON-1-12-33-102
ANDREWS-57-79-85
ANSLEY-23
ARDIS-67-79
ARMSTRONG-13
ARNO-33
ATKINS-ADKINS-59
ATKINSON-ADKINSON-7-13-59-
    67-102-103
AUSTIN-1-13-24-85
AVERY-33
AYDELOTTE-51-67-79

BADLEY-13
BAILEY-BALEY-BAYLEY-1-14-24-
    67-86
BAKER-63-68-77-78-79
BALL-85-99
BALLARD-1-7-24-39-34-78
BANKS-1-13-86
BANNISTER-29-67
BARCABUS-29
BARNES-103
BARNCASTLE-86
BASSETT-60-63-70
BARTLEY-7
BAYNUM-77
BAYNS-1
BASHAW-85
BEACHBOARD-80
BEAGLOW-86
BEAUCHAMP-33-34-43-44-46-
    47-51-63-68-85
BEARD-1-7
BEEL-43
BEEDLE-77
BEDSWORTH-BETSWORTH-13-33
BELL-13-24-29-39-46-77-78-
    79
BENNETT-2-13-80-85-94-96
BENSON-BENSTON-7-29-33-39-
    46-47-51-64-77-99
BEVANS-59-70-103
BETHARDS-60-64-78
BIGLAND-BEAGLAND-86

BING-1
BIRD-13-39
BISHOP-55-60-64-94-95-96
BITTS-63
BLADES-46-51
BLAKE-29-60-85-94-79
BLOODSWORTH-33
BLIZZARD-63-64
BLUITT-86
BONNAWILL-79
BOSTON-29-34-44-46-47-51
BOUNDS-1-7
BOZMAN-24-29-33
BOTHAM-13
BOWEN-55-67-77-78-96-103
BOWLAND-103
BRADFORD-55-67-68-73-77-78
BRERETON-1
BRATTAN-59-76-78-95
BRADCHER-BRASURE-30-67-68-70-
    79-84
BRIDDLE-60-63-68
BREWINGTON-86
BREVARD-67
BRINKLEY-7
BRITTINGHAM-51-60-63-67-70-79-
    84-85-95-96
BRITT-99
BROUGHTON-34-44-46-47
BRUFF-46
BRUMBLY-BRUMBLE-59-63-79
BROWN-2-13-29-85-86-99
BUCHANNON-51
BURBAGE-55
BURSHALL-51
BURNETT-51
BUTLER-99
CAMERON-85
CALLAHAN-2
CAMBALL-CAMPBELL-24-64-68-98
CAMBRIDGE-64
CALDWELL-86
CANNON-8
CANTWELL-14-24
CARMAN-87
CARBERRY-87
CARMICHAEL-13
CATHELL-87
CATHERWOOD-94
CATLIN-CATLING-34
CAREY-68-69-85-86-87
CARTER-85
CAVANAUGH-24
CHANDLER-40
CHAILLE-55-64-85-99
CHAMBERS-2-94
CHITTAM-2
CHANE-2

CHANEY-33
CHRISTA-55
CLARK-68
CLAYWELL-64-90-98
CLIFTON-99
CILPIN-85
CLUFF-47
CLOGG-85-90
CLAUDS-85
COFFIN-78
COHOON-34-68
COLBERT-34
COLLIER-7-8-14-68-70
COLLICK-98
COLLINS-2-44-55-68-78-85
COLLETT-2
CONNERLY-14
CONNER-40-78-85-98
CONWAY-8-34
COOKSEY-87
COPEES-99
CORKWELL-64
CORBAN-99
COTTINGHAM-34-64-98-99
CORDRAY-7-14-64-70-78
COOPER-14
COTTMAN-2-7-47
COULBOURN-39-40-44
COSTON-47-85-98
COWLEY-85
COVINGTON-7-24-70-99
COX-2-39-44-78-87-74
CRAFORD-85
CROCKETT-8
CROSWELL-39-40
CROPPER-CRAPPER-55-68-70-
    78-99
CROUCH-87
CULLEN-8-34-39-40
CULVER-14-87
CURLIS-68
CURREN-78-94
CURTIS -34
CUTLER-64

DAGSWORTHY-72
DAILY-DALEY-3-89
DALE-62-68-69-70-99
DALIFOUNT-68
DARCUS-40
DARBY-14
DASHIELL-2-3-8-9-14-24-89
DAUGHTY-24
DAUGHERTY-40
DAVIS-14-24-30-34-47-52-55-
    56-61-62-64-65-69-70-82-
    85-87-88-89-98
DAWSEY-34
DEAN-9-47

DEER-47
DENNIS-3-52-65-71-88-93-94-
    98-99
DENSTON-30-100-101
DENWOOD-9-33
DERRICKSON-35
DEVORIX-98
DIES-30-40-
DIKES-88-89
DICKERSON-8-52-65-82-99
DIGNER-33
DISHEROON-2-3-88-89
DIOR-69
DIXON-34-85-98-100
DOCKERY-2
DOUGLAS-8
DORITHY-8-9
DONOHO-8-101
DOREY-35
DONOVAN-62
DORWICK-47
DRAGOO-72
DRISKELL-89
DRUMMOND-100-101
DORMAN-2-14-30-47-89-93-94-
    98-99-101
DRYDEN-DREDDEN-30-47-62-65-
    98-100
DUBBERLY-55-100
DUER-85-94
DUNCAN-55-56-62-72
DUBLING-47
DUKES-82-99-101
DUNN-8-14
DUTTON-3-14
DURHAM-30
DYKES-44
DYMOCK-3-93

ELLENSWORTH-9
ELLIOTT-93
ELZEY-3-24-30-32
ENNIS-56-65-98-99
ESHUM-ESHAM-65-101
EVANS-9-24-40-44-56-65-72
ELLIS-15-52-98-99

FALL-69
FARLOW-65
FASSITT-56-69-72-94
FAULKINOR-69
FISHER-47
FITZGERALD-3-56
FLETCHER-15
FLINT-93
FLEMMING-47-101
FLEULLIN-9
FOLLIN-15
FOOKS-65-93

FOUNTAIN-35-65
FOURDS-47
FOURTON-30
FOWLER-3-14
FRANKLIN-69-72
FRAZIER-15
FREENEY-93
FULLERTON-9
FURBUSH-9
FURNISS-30-47

GAGE-82
GALE-3-9-15-24-32
GAME-9
GARLAND-35
GATRO-32
GAULT-6
GIBSON-15-35-25
GILES-15-44-64
GILLETTE-52
GIBB-GIBBS-93-101-82
GILLIS-3-15-24-25-30
GIVAN-GIVANS-30-65-82-93-94
GLADDING-93
GLASGOE-56
GLASS-56-64
GLASTER-15
GODFREY-56-65-66-69-70
GODDARD-15
GORDY-93
GORNWELL-99
GOSLEE-3-9-15
GRAHAM-9-15
GRIFFITH-3
GREEN-9-56-70
GRIFFIN-56-65-69
GREER-93-99
GRAVENOR-15
GRAY-65-69-70
GULLETT-3
GUNBY-3-15-40
GUNDY-69
GUNN-94
GURLEY-93
GURNEY-35
GUTHRY-82-94-101

HADDER-76
HAILES-HALE-30-93-99
HALL-25-35-48-64-77-94
HAMBLEN-64-70-76-77
HANCOCK-52-56-69-77-81-83
HANDY-4-10-16-35-40-64-93-
    94-98-101
HAMMOND-56-65-77-83-99-101
HARRISON-15-69-70
HARDY-15
HARRIS-3-10-15-47-48-92-
    94-101

HASTINGS-16
HAYMAN-4-92-93
HATH-25-30-48
HAYNIE-10-16-17
HAYWARD-25-48-64-94
HAYLEY-44
HAZZARD-76
HEARN-16-40-64-93-94-
  (HERON)
HEATH-64
HENDERSON-4-16-40-52-56-65-70-
    76-81-98
HENRY-16-44-76-94
HENSON-92
HICKMAN-75
HICKS-23
HILL-52-56-69-70-81-82-83
HILMAN-3-4-
HITCH-4-16-17
HOBBS-16-25-92-
HODGE-56
HOLBROOK-3-10
HOLLAND-30-40-47-56-69-82-
    92-101
HOLLOWAY-64-69-70-77
HOOK-98
HOPKINS-10-25-40-76-82-94
HOPEWELL-35
HORNER-25
HORSEY-4-16-30-35-40-92
HOSHIER-56
HOWARD-16-32-35-76-92
HOZIER-64-65-76
HOUSTON-52-64-81-92
HUDSON-52-56-64-70-75-76-77-
    82-83-94-101
HOWARTH-35
HUNT-101
HUTCHINS-44
HUETT-81
HULL-15
HUGHES-10-98
HUFFINGTON-16
HUMPHRIES-4-16
HUST-16
HYLAND-25

INGERSOLL-4
INGOLSON-93
IRONSHIRE-76
IRVING-17-29-30

JACKSON-10-17-32
JAMES-10-17-91-93
JARMAN-56-65-76
JARVIS-25
JEANNOR-4
JENKINS-4

JOHNSON-17-35-36-41-53-56-57-
    76-81-82-93-98-101
JONES-4-10-17-25-30-32-35-36-
    52-53-56-57-65-76-81-82

KENNERLY-18
KENNETT-75-76
DERR-31
KERSEY-18-44
DELLY-101
KIBBLE-4
KILBY-4
KILLAM-KILLUM-KELLAM-17-31-36-
    41-82-83-94
KILLEY-KILEY-26-66
KING-10-18-25-30-31-36-48-75
KIRBY-75
KNIGHT-4-48
KNISSE-41
KNOX-57-75

LAMBDEN-82-94-101
LANDEN-10-18-31-36
LANE-53
LANK-4-18-91
LAMBERSON-53-55-75-82-91
LANKFORD-18-31-36-41-101
LATCHUM-75
LARRIMORE-10
LAWES-LAWS-26-31-66-67
LAWSON-41
LAYFIELD-4-31-36-53-82-
    91-101
LAWRENCE-4-75
LEACH-36
LEATHERBURY-4-10-18
LECOUNT-94
LENDALL-75
LEONARD-4-91-101
LEVINS-4
LEWIS-53-66-75
LIBBY-10
LINGO-75
LINDSAY-36-82
LINTON-41
LISTER-36
LIVINGSTON-44-91
LLOYD-18
LOCKWOOD-75
LOKEY-91-101
LOWE-LOWES-4-10-18-91
LONG-31-32-36-41-48-53-
    57-75-94
LORD-18
LOWRY-66
LURTEN-4
LYNCH-70-75

MADDUX-5-10-32-36-48-81-
    90-91-93-101

MAGEE-67
MALONE-5
MARSH-73-98
MARSHALL-36-37-44-45-53-57-73
MASON-41-53-67-73
MASSEY-73-75
MARTIN-26-67-80-82-95-94-97-
    98-101
MATHIAS-31
MARCHANT-44-45 (MERCHANT)
MATTHEWS-10-31-44-45-48
MEARS-91
MELVIN-53-81
MARCHMENT-57-98
MELSON-19-73-91
MERRILL-41-48-53-73-80-81-97
MESSICK-11-18
MIFFLIN-53-80
MILBOURN-36-37-41-44-45-80
MILES-5-26-31-36-37-41-48-
    49-101
MILLER-73-75
MILLICAN-37
MILLS-26-45-48-53-54-73-75-
    90-92
MISTER-41
MONCURS-32
MONTGOMERY-41
MITCHELL-5-31-37-48-67-70-73-
    75-90
MOOR-MOORE-11-18-36-37-41-
    48-70
MORRIS-5-18-57-67-73-92-95-
    97-98
MUIR-26-31
MULLING-95
MUMFORD-57-67-73-75-98
MUNGAR-92
MURPHY-MURFEE-18-90
MURRAY-31-53-67-75-90-95

McALLEN-101
McBRYDE-McBRIDE-5-10-92
McCAN-48
McCally-97
McCENNY-41
McClemmy-19-26-32
McCLANNEN-19
McCLELLAN-19
McCLAIN-36
McCLISH-67
McCLESTER-10-11-19
McCOMB-26
McCREADY-44-45-53
McCORMICK=73
McCRAY-73
McCUDDY-101
McDANIEL-67
McDonald-36
McDorman- 26

McGEE-90-67-92
McGLAMERY-90
McGRATH-26-31
McHENRY-81
McINTYRE-10-11
McLALLEN-79
McLEARY-5
McLAUGHLEN-5
McLALLY-19
McNAB-91
McMASTERS-53
McNEILLE-75
McNIDER-45
McVEY-26

NELMS-5
NELSON-19
NEWMAN-5-26
NICHOLS-11
NICHOLSON-19
NIGHT-26
NOBLE-26
NORTH-11
NUTTER-5-19

OKEY-54
OLLIPHANT-91
ORPHANT-5
OWENS-OWINS-26-91-102
OUTTEN-37-57-60-102
OTWELL-102

PADEN-48
PANK-91
PARKER-5-26-32-60-74-81-
    80-91-97
PARKES-PARKS-26-37-41-54
PATEY-70
PARREMORE-20-41-80
PARIS-11
PARRADICE-54
PARSONS-60-61-62-91
PATTERSON-54
PAUL-41
PATRICK-81
PEACOCK-48
PENNIWILL-57-58-73-60
PAYNE-60-81
PEPPER-74-80-97
PERDUE-90-91
PETTIGRU-80
PGEBUS-26
PHILLIPS-19-20-91
PILCHER-PILCHARD-48-54-80
PIPER-20
PITT-74
POLK-5-6-20-31-32
POLLITT-5-31-33-62-90-97

PORTER-11-20-49-54-57-60-91-95
POINTER-POYNTER-57-61-97
POTTER-37
POSTLEY-73
POUNDERS-60
POWELL-48-49-60-70-74-102
PRICE-5-32-81-95
PRIDEAUX-57-74
PRYOR-37
PRUITT-91
PULLET-5
PUCKAM-90
PURKINS-37-48-54-57-74
PURNELL-57-58-60-70-71-73-74-
    81-95-97
PUZEY-PEWSY-32-49-102

QUILLAN-74
QUINN-90
QUINTON-20-54-58-80-85-102

RAIN-58-63-97
RANDALL-95
RANKIN-75
RATCLIFFE-RACKLIFFE-58-62-74-78
READ-REED-REID-11-26-27-63-80-
    102
REEDY-20
RECORDS-20
REESE-49
REDDIN-REDDING-37-54-102
REDDISH-6
RENCHER-6-20
REVELL-32-49
REYNALDS-RENALDS-58
RICHARDS-6-58-78-102
RICHARDSON-58-62-63-86-96-98
RICHEY-11-49
RIDER-11
RIGGIN-41-45-49-80-86-102
RIGGS-90
RIBSBY-58
RHOADS-20
ROACH-37-41-54-90-102
ROBINS-62-78-80-86-95-96-97-102
ROBINSON-54-63-80-86-90-95
ROAN-78
ROCK-6
ROBERTSON-11-20-30-37
ROBERTS-20-27-63-90
RODNEY-80
ROE-27
ROLE-20
ROLAND-78
ROSE-20
ROSS-95
ROWLEY-80
ROOKE-90

ROUNDS-32-58-63-78
RUARK-58-62-86-102
RUMMER-20
RUMBLEY-11
RUSSELL-11-20
RYAN-RION-70-78
RYLEY-75-78-86

SANDERS-58
SADLER-84
SASSER-27
SAWYER-96
SAVAGE-96
SCARBROUGH-80-94-96-97
SCHOOLFIELD-37-45-54-78-96
SCOTT-12-61-102
SCROGGIN-21-87
SEADY-88
SEBRON-21
SELBY-54-58-59-63-78-79-80-
    84-95-96-102
SEARS-78
SHEPHERD-33
SHELTON-27
SHILES-6
SHIPHAM-32
SHORES-27
SHOCKLEY-63-86-87-88
SHOWELL-79-86
SIMS-27
SIRMAN-6-12
SKINNER-6
SKIRVING-27
SLOAN-49
SLOCOMB-84
SLOSS-27
SMITH-2-21-27-32-37-49-54-
    58-59-63-70-78-86-94
SMALL-45
SMOCK-69-63-78-79
SLAUGHTER-61
SMULLEN-49-87
SNEAD-79-84
SOCKWELL-6
SPENCE-84-95-96-97
SPRING-97
STANFORD-6-88-21-32
STEEL-96-97
SPEAR-SPEIRS-6397
STARLING-STERLING-21-42-54
STEWART-STUART-27-32-71-78-
    79-80
STEPHENSON-STEVENSON-54-59-
    78-79-80-84-96-97
STONE-21
STEVENS-6-21-49-59-79-80-
    94
STRAWBRIDGE-32-33
STURGIS-6-63-80-84-86-88
    95-97

SUDLER-37
SUMMERS-SOMERS-38-42-49
SWIFT-27

TARR-61-83-96
TAYLOR-6-21-22-32-45-54-59-70-
    71-83-84-88-96-100
TAWS-42
TEAGUE-54-96
THOMAS-42
THOMPSON-59
TIGNEL-88
TINGLE-61-71
TINDALL-54-61-83
TILGHMAN-32-38-49-50-100-102
TREHEARN-38
TRAIN-21
TIMMONS-27-61-70-71-
TOWNSEND-12-54-59-61-66-70-71-
    83-94-96-100-102
THORNS-21
TOADVINE-88
TRADER-TRAYDER-21-88
TRUITT-59-61-66-71-83-94-96
TUBBS-71
TULLY-12-21-23
TULL-21-38-45-49-50-71-83-88
TUNNELL-83
TURNER-61-66-71-83-88-100
TURPIN-21-38
TWIGGS-88
TWILLEY-21-61
TYLOR-42-54

VANCE-89
VANDOM-83
VAUGHN-22
VEAZEY-83-84-100
VENABLES-6-7-22-88
VESSELS-38
VESTRY-100
VEAZEY-83-84-100
VICTOR-66
VIGEROUS-71
VICASS-22
VINSON-22-61-88-89

WABERTON-7
WAGGAMEN-23-27-29-32-33
WALKER-59
WALLER-7-12-22-23-28
WALLACE-28-29
WALSTON-28-32-89-91
WALTON-32-84
WARD-42-43-45-46-50-89-100
WARRINGTON-73
WARWICK-50
WARREN-73
WATERS-7-22-38-39-50-70-73-
    94-96

WADDEY-45
WEBSTER-28-29
WALES-12-23
WELLS-100
WETMAN-46
WEST-22-39-96
WEATHERLY-22-23
WESTMAN-7
WHEALOR-WHEELER-46-66
WHEATLEY-39-43
WHITTINGTON-42-43-71
WATTS-72
WHITNEY-28
WHETHIAR-33
WHITTINGHAM-33
WHITTINGTON-22
WHORTON-23
WHALEN-7
WILLETT-84
WILLIN-7-12
WILKINS-28-66
WILLIS-32-66-89-101
WILLIAMS-7-23-29-38-39-43-
    66-71-72-100
WINDER-7-22-32-89
WINRIGHT-12
WINGATE-28
WINSOR-WINDSOR-12-28-29-66
WILSON-22-23-27-28-32-33-38
    39-43-46-50-59-70-89
WHITE-28-42-46-50-66-73-84
WOOLFORD-28
WOOD-46
WONNELL-100
WRILEY-7
WRIGHT-7-23-28-66-96

YELVERTON-80-95-97
YOUNG-52-73

www.ingramcontent.com/pod-product-compliance
Lightning Source LLC
LaVergne TN
LVHW091601060526
838200LV00036B/942